PURPOSE, PAIN'S PROMISE

Finding Purpose through Painful Experiences

LYNETTE LEWIS

Dedication

This book is dedicated to all the women who have endured the pain of their past and survived to see their life blossom into *purpose*. Each episode of your life, no matter how painful, prepares you for your destiny and purpose. I thank God for reassuring me that the scars on my body from the abuse of the past, are just a reminder of when life tried to kill me but couldn't. As I continue to mature in age and look back over my life, the scripture found in Romans 8:28 is much clearer to me now: *"And we know that all things work together for good to them that love God, to them who are the called according to his purpose"*. The aftermath of our pain reveals our purpose. Keep living, keep learning, and keep growing to reveal the purposeful life God intends for you to live, in spite of the *pain*.

Table of Contents

Acknowledgements

First, I give honor to God, who loved me enough to carry me through every painful storm in my life and graced me for this journey into purpose.

I want to thank my wonderful husband, Larry Lewis, who encouraged me through the process of writing this book and standing in my truth. I love you so very much and thank God for your calm demeanor, non-judgmental ways and support of everything I set my hands to do. God truly saved the best for last.

To my sons, Derrick D. Joyce and Christopher D. Joyce, thank you for your love and support throughout the years. You embraced all my endeavors and stood with me when I struggled through wavering emotions, difficult relationships and my journey in life. I am so very proud of the great men of God you have become and how you are endeavoring to bring your best self to every situation. I love you both very much. To my daughter in love, Latia Joyce, grandchildren, Ahmad Nealy, Derrick Joyce, Jr., Jeriah Joyce, Amariah Joyce and great-grandson, Jaevion Nealy, I love you all.

To my best friend and sister in Christ, Barbara Prioleau, who went home to be with the Lord on September 25, 2018, thank you for always standing by my side throughout the years with your unconditional love and friendship. You were indeed a true sister to me and I cherished our relationship over those 36 years. I loved and appreciated you greatly. To Sheila Dykes, Gloria Myers, Vivian Gibson and Cathy Salley, my other sisters in Christ whom have stood by me over the years and loved me for who I am. Thanks for your support and I love you ladies to life.

To my family, sister, brothers, nieces, nephews, and cousins thank you for your impact on my life in both large and small ways. I am the woman I am today partly because of all I've experienced with family members both past and present. I love you all and pray that you all live your best lives and passionately pursue your purpose.

To my We Are Women in Business sisters, founded by Coach J. Dianne Tribble and Quen Sams, thank you so very much for your inspiration to stretch and dream big. It is because of you, I felt empowered to start my business, Purpose Made Alive, LLC, and pursue other meaningful endeavors to walk in my purpose. Thank you also for allowing me to serve as your Chaplin and enjoy the sisterhood in a warm and welcoming environment created by a wonderful group of professional women. Love you ladies very much.

To all my spiritual fathers and mothers, thank you for pouring into my life over the years and I pray God will abundantly reward you for the seeds you've sown. I would not be the woman I am today without your unique spiritual deposits. Pilgrim Baptist Church, Eastside Baptist Church and Lord of The Harvest CFC – all of Charleston SC, New Birth Missionary Baptist Church and New Life Church – of Atlanta GA, Impact Church – Jacksonville FL.

Introduction

The journey of life, we all have one and no one can tell the story of your journey like you can. One thing I've come to know for sure and that is God would have all His children free of guilt and shame and to understand that no matter what this life brings our way, we can embrace it as a lesson in our education of survival. God wants us to be transparent and live authentic lives, which often is overshadowed by our desire to protect our reputation, guard ourselves from possible rejection, and the need to cover up flaws with the mask of perfection. Interestingly, the one who holds our lives in the palm of His hands already knows our story and if He's able to handle it then why are we so concerned about how others will see us. In writing this book, I was confronted with the decision to tell some of my story, but not all, because of the fear of what people may think. God made it clear to me that this is a transformational moment in my life and the whole truth, nothing but the truth, would suffice in order to go to the next level. There comes a time when one must say, "I've got to own my past and be brave enough to reveal and speak my truth and if it causes people to judge me and/or no longer want to be my friend or associate, then so be it." The good, the bad and the ugly makes up my journey and I would say that's probably true for all of us. My heart's desire is that something shared in this book will unlock buried secrets in others and give them the courage to speak their truth so that the world can be filled with transparent authentic people, each understanding that we are all vulnerable in some areas, but it connects us to all the other humans who are also vulnerable in similar areas as well. I truly believe that my growth over the years was fueled by the lessons learned from my failures, bad decisions, successes and triumphs. It has all worked together for my good, even when it didn't feel that way and I thought I wouldn't come out on the other side of the pain, but I did. I can no longer be ashamed or silent about things that make up my journey because that's fertile ground for the enemy to sow his seeds of guilt, shame and thoughts of I'm less than. Well no longer. This is the season for change and it starts with emptying myself of every ugly memory, shameful act or decision, and every desire to do only what pleases others without thought of what would change the world around me. I believe God wants us to live out our purpose to make a difference in the lives of others and not concern ourselves with what will only look good to others. When I think back over my life, all I can say is, if it had not been for the Lord who was on my side, where would I be. God has brought me through so many things and the woman that I am now and the woman that God is still molding me to be is all because of who He is and what He has done and is doing in and through my life. This is my story, *Purpose, Pain's Promise*.

The Early Days & Beyond

I could feel the warm blood running down the side of my face and the excruciating pain coming from my forehead. The first memory I can recall in life is one of pain. It was my first memory, but it would not be the last because pain is something I can say I've had my share of over the years but by the mercy and grace of God, I am still here to tell the story. At the time of this incident, I couldn't have been more than 18 months - 2 years old as I see it in my mind's eye. I was running around just as happy as I could be, with my diaper on and my little fat legs jumping freely. What happened you may ask? Well, my older brother, who was only 4 years older than me, hit me in the head with a brick. I can't imagine what would have caused him to do this, but it was just the first of many such incidents because as I recall, he was just evil like that and especially with me. I was never sure why he targeted me, but this incident was just the beginning of years of physical abuse from someone who should have been protecting me as their little sister. When I was around four years old another event occurred, which had a lasting impact on my life. My brother beat our new little puppy to death and threw his dead body into my arms. This was such a horrifying experience for me that I buried the memory in my subconscious mind and didn't remember it until years later when I had an unusual encounter with a co-worker while working for a life insurance company in Charleston SC. Here's what happened. Being a Christian, I would leave Chick tracts (miniature comic books with a Christian message) in the public restroom at work. One day I left one related to domestic violence and it apparently offended one of my co-workers. She complained to my office manager, who called me into her office since she suspected it was me who left the tract in the restroom. When my manager explained to me the issue, I confessed that I had placed the tract in the restroom but immediately apologized and expressed no intent to offend this co-worker, who apparently was in an abusive relationship. When I left her office I immediately reached out to my co-worker and apologized and again expressed no intent to offend her. Well, during this apology, I started to share with her how I had been abused by my brother while growing up and I understood physical abuse. As I began to share with her some of the things he had done to me, the memory of him throwing our dead puppy into my arms flooded into my memory and I just lost it. I began to cry uncontrollably and had to return to my manager's office so as not to disturb the other staff members. I was in such hysterics that my manager asked a co-worker to drive me home. While we were riding home, the Lord spoke to me clearly that I needed to call my brother and ask him to forgive me for hating him because of the things he did. In my heart, I was like, "God, you must be kidding. Me ask him to forgive me when he should be begging my forgiveness?" Our God is unique in how He handles things, which is often contrary to our ways. I was finally able to gather myself and make the call when I got home because I knew it was better to be obedient even if I didn't understand it. I placed the call and when my brother answered the phone I basically told him that God wanted me to call and ask him to forgive me for hating him for so many years because of how he treated me. I also told him that I had just remembered what he had done to our little puppy. By then I was crying again, and he immediately started crying and asking me to forgive him. Wow, what a shocker. God knew it was him who really needed to ask for forgiveness, but he would have never did it on his own and it would take me initiating that exchange in order to open the door for forgiveness. Even though at the time I said I forgave him, my story will later reveal that this was not the case, but I managed to carry out that act of obedience to the extent that I could at the time. Recalling that incident explained why I always had a fear of dogs and didn't initially understand why, but now I know. Still at this time in my life, at the age of 63 years old, I can't bring myself to touch a dog, although I don't want any harm to come to them. I seem to always have a soft spot in my heart for dogs when I see them, but I just can't bring myself to touch one. This is an area I'm still working through and one day expect to have the needed breakthrough, just like I've experienced in other areas of my life.

I understand today that the enemy wanted to take me out at an early age either physically or mentally because he had a peek into my future. He knew I would be a possible threat to the kingdom of darkness because I would lead souls to the Lord through community outreach ministry and the preaching of the gospel. He meant every evil experience of abuse for my destruction, but God allowed it for my good. You see that's how the enemy works. He will use any and everyone around you to either destroy you in death or torture you enough until you feel like dying. The Word of God tells us that the "thief comes only to steal, kill and destroy" but thank God, Jesus came that we might have life and have it more abundantly. Although our lives have a lot of twists and turns, it is a journey that God has already witnessed, approved and prepared us to handle. The abundant life was something I longed for throughout my life and oftentimes it seemed too hard to grasp and experience, but I never gave up continuing to seek it, sometimes in the wrong places,

7

in the wrong ways and with the wrong motives. Thanks be to God, however, there is still life to be lived and that was just the beginning with several chapters yet to walk through, leading up to that final chapter and the end.

I was born Lynette Williams in Jacksonville, Florida on February 4, 1955, at Brewster Hospital and was the third of my mother's seven children. I don't like the fact that my mother did not give me a middle name because it's always an issue when filling out forms and applications, which often requires a middle initial. When my mother gave birth to me, unfortunately she was not married so I was never quite confident of the identity of my real father. Sadly enough, however, the man whom my mother identified as the father of my oldest brother, my sister and me, was a married man. Oh my. Yes, it pains me to even think of that now as I write this story. How painful that must have been for his wife, if she knew; however, even more troubling is what was going on with my mother at the time, for her to allow herself to be involved with a married man and give birth to three children because of it. I'm told this was more common place than one would think, even with men in the church on the deacon board and even in the pulpit. They would try to take care of two, and sometimes three families, as if God didn't see it all, in addition to some of the nosy members of the congregation. Regardless of it being commonplace, I would rather have a different story for my beginning, but as I often say, it is what it is.

By the time my mother had her fifth child, she was finally married to a man 20 years her senior, whom we were told fancied her even as a young girl at the tender age of 12. He waited for her to be old enough to marry, but she apparently held out on him for several years, because she didn't have her first child until she was 26 years old and her fifth when she was 34. She gave birth to three children from the married man and then the next three were with the man she married. However, she listed the man 20 years her senior on all our birth certificates. I could never understand it, because they were not married or even together when we were born. I imagine she knew it was safer to list him than the real father. I still must give her some credit for waiting to have children until after she graduated from cosmetology school and spent time in Philadelphia PA singing with Clara Ward and the Ward singers, a famous gospel group from the 1940's and 1950's. Since my oldest brother was born in 1951, I can only speculate that's when my mother left the group, which later went on to attain great fame in the gospel singing arena throughout the 50's with the original group dissolving in 1958. A new group formed shortly thereafter and actually sang at the Apollo Theater in 1963. My mother could really sing, and she often sang the song "How I Got Over", which is one of the songs that made the Ward singers famous. She didn't hesitate to make sure people knew how well she sang, especially when she visited churches and sang along during the congregational hymns. She would sing louder than anyone else, but her voice was so strong and powerful everyone would turn around and look in her direction. My brothers, sister and I would be so embarrassed, but thanked God that at least she sounded really good. I had always said as a young girl, I wish I could sing like my mother, but none of my siblings or me received the gift. When I became an adult, I was proud of how well she could sing and especially recall the time she visited with me and my family in Charleston SC, after the birth of my second son. As usual, we attended church on Sunday during her visit and as always, she sang loud during the singing portion of the service. This time I was very proud of her singing and was thrilled when people came up to her afterwards to tell her how much they enjoyed her voice and how well she could sing. I sometimes think what it would have been like if she pursued a singing career. She had the voice for sure, but I guess it was not meant to be.

By the time my mother married, I was around four years old, and I recall that my step-father was very quiet during the week, but over the weekends, he was a different person. It would start on Friday nights when he got paid, and he would go out drinking with his buddies all weekend. He was a tall thin dark-skinned man who was rather handsome and always clean in appearance. He often wore starched beige khaki pants and starched white shirts, with a white tee shirt underneath. My mother on the other hand was a short dark-skinned woman, who was very much overweight, earning her the nickname of "pig" by her best friend, Harry Mae, whose nickname was "Road" because she was always on the road going somewhere. I used to wonder what attracted my stepfather to my mother because of the difference in their sizes and age, but I've often heard that a lot of thin men like larger women, so for those two, it was true. My mother hated the fact that he drank, and they would always argue about It, but I don't ever recall him ever being physically or verbally abusive to her. Apparently, he spent more money on drinking than he should have, and she would be short on money needed to take care of the household.

It's amazing how there are certain things you can remember from your childhood and then there are other things you can't recall at all. I do remember my mother still being in contact with the married man even after she married, and he would give her money when she needed it to supplement her income because I don't believe he paid actual child support in those days.

This married man owned his own barbershop on 8th street in Jacksonville and was considered an upstanding businessman in the community but obviously not such a great husband. Sadly enough, this was the story of several men in those days. Their wives either didn't know or pretended not to know anything about what they were doing outside of the home. I just hated the fact that I could not publicly identify this man as my father; on my birth certificate, my mother listed the man she knew and later married. It is the same to this day. My real father was a light-skinned, tall man and very handsome. After we moved to Philadelphia and returned to Jacksonville for visits and funerals, he would visit us sometimes at my auntie's house. As I recall, he would only stand at the door and speak to us in the doorway of her house instead of coming in and sitting down. I guess he didn't want anyone to see his car there for any length of time. My auntie lived in the Durkeyville projects off Davis Street back then and although her house had those cement floors that were always cold even in the summer time, we loved visiting her and my cousins. It was a lot of us when we got together. Those of us who didn't have a bed to sleep in, which was most of us, slept on the floor. My mother had six children at the time and auntie Viola had five living at home but had a total of eight children altogether. So, eleven children and two adults made for a crowded, but happy time together. My aunt and mother would stay up talking and laughing and reminiscing about days past and catching up on other family news or should I say gossip. They were closer to each other than they were with their other siblings. It reminds me of the "haves and the have nots" family dynamics and you can guess which ones we were, the "have nots", but we got along just fine. The other side of the family weren't exactly rich, but most of them were married and their children and grandchildren went to college, not to mention they had their own homes and none of them lived in the projects. I used to envy some of my cousins because they usually had nicer clothes than we did, and one of them had a doll house and a piano. Growing up I always thought that girls who had those large doll houses were wealthy. Owning a doll house was one of my greatest desires growing up but I never received one and still to this day sometimes think I should buy one just to satisfy that old desire never fulfilled. I still haven't bought one, even though I can now afford one. I'll see if the desire compels me to do so before I leave this earth.

My mother gave birth to her sixth child, a boy, when she was 36 years old. At the time I was six, my sister was seven and my oldest brother was ten. Later that year my sister took ill and I remember one morning, she could not walk or get out of bed because she was so weak. We slept in the same room, and I remember being very scared and cried uncontrollably at the thought of my sister not being able to walk. We were very close growing up since we were only one year apart in age. My mother took her to the hospital and they admitted her with the diagnosis of rheumatic heart failure. It was a very scary time for me since I didn't want my sister to die and this was the first time that we were apart from each other. She was in the hospital for several days and unfortunately it extended over the weekend. Well, the weekend was not a fun place around our house because my stepfather was always drunk and acted differently than he did during the week. One night I recall that it was dark and rainy outside, and he was drinking. I stayed in my room since my mother was at the hospital with my sister. The next thing I recall is that my stepfather had come into my room and was laying on top of me and I could smell that alcohol on his breath, which made me want to throw up. To this day, I can't tolerate the smell of alcohol on someone's breathe. He was so heavy, and I was so scared and in shock because this was the first time anything like this had ever happened. I was six years old. I don't know if I blacked out or if I just buried the memory of the experience in my subconscious mind but when I came to, I ached all over. I don't know if it was from heartache because of what happened or actual pain. However, I never mentioned this to my mother and from that day forward my relationship changed with my stepfather in a very weird way. It seemed as if he was always favoring me in some way and being one of six children, I started to like that. Strange as I look back on it, but I am sure there is some psychological explanation for it. Abuse has a way of impacting you in ways you don't expect and can't explain. If anything, I should have tried to get as far away from him as possible, but could it have been at that young age I was exhibiting a desire to be loved, even if it was perverted and I didn't realize it. The need for love is just a basic emotion, but we all need it and unfortunately sometimes will do anything to try to get it. I am not saying in no way what happened was a demonstration of love, but after the fact, the misguided attention may have appeared to my young mind as love. Satan tries to negatively impact our lives even as little children because we are most vulnerable during those years. He wants to set us up for failure in the future, but God turns what he meant for evil for our good, not that the event was good, but God can get a deliverance out of it, and later in my life, He did just that.

Well, my sister got better and came home from the hospital and my stepfather never came into my room again. However, one weekend, he was drinking and laying across the bed with my youngest brother, Donald, who was still a baby, and he fell asleep with a cigarette in his hand. He used to smoke those Lucky Strike cigarettes with no filter. The bed caught fire with him and my baby brother in it, yet both asleep. It was the grace of God that allowed my mother to rescue them both and the house didn't burn down, although the mattress was ruined. My mother was so angry and kept saying that this was the last straw. She could not take his drinking anymore and that she was going to leave him and move back to Philadelphia, where she spent a few years singing when she was younger. She had always told us that if my grandmother ever died she would move back to Philadelphia because there was no reason for her to stay in Jacksonville. Well my grandmother had passed away the year before, but she didn't make the move at that time and she was now married. I supposed this straw broke the camel's back. So, in 1963, when I was eight years old my mother moved our family, minus my stepfather, to Philadelphia PA. I will never forget that time in our lives.

The Move to Philadelphia

It was in May of 1963, when my mother packed up all our belongings and we moved to Philadelphia. I remember her receiving some money from the married man, my father, to help pay for the trip. My mother was a very strong woman to leave her friends and family and move to a city where she no longer knew anyone without a place to stay or a job. When we arrived, we thought we were going to freeze to death since it was still cold in May in Philadelphia, but when we left Jacksonville it was hot, almost like summer time. Since we didn't have a place to stay, we lived in a hotel until my oldest brother dropped a water balloon out the window and it hit someone walking by, which led to the hotel kicking us out. We didn't have anywhere to go but my mother met these three sisters who lived together, and they invited us to stay at their house for a few days until my mother could make other arrangements. We were homeless. I believe this is why I have such a burden for the homeless to this day. I thank God that people were much more hospitable in those days, much more so than what we see today. Taking in a woman with six kids, that's a rare kind of hospitality, even for a few days.

A few weeks later, my mother met an older lady who lived alone, and she invited us to come and stay with her until my mother could find a place of her own. Her house was very nice. I remember really enjoying our stay there. She had lace scarfs on her tables and we all sat down to eat dinner together at a long dining room table. She would not let us drink anything until we finished our food. We used to have iced tea and Kool-Aid, which was a treat for us since we only drank those beverages when my mother had extra money, or it was a special occasion, otherwise it was water, water, and water. We stayed with her for several weeks. Thankfully, it was summer by then and we didn't need to worry about going to school yet. This experience of not having an actual home causes me to appreciate the plight of our homeless brothers and sisters because we were right there and know what that's like. These wonderful ladies really extended themselves to open their homes to a woman with six children, whom they didn't really know that well. God is good, and he will place people in our path that are selfless and don't mind extending a helping hand to those in need. That set the tone for me leading a life of service to others because, but for the grace of God, it could be me in need because we were those people at one time, yet we had people to help us.

Finally, we were able to get our own place in North Philadelphia, a row house, which was new to us since we didn't have those in Jacksonville. I remember when I was in the fourth grade, the first year we were there, the kids at school teased me because of my southern accent. I hated to read out loud in class because all the kids would laugh and pretend to talk like me. I always loved school though and enjoyed learning even though I was a year ahead throughout my school career because I skipped Kindergarten and went directly into first grade at the age of five. I did well in school despite their teasing but really wanted to make friends with someone and be accepted by the other kids.

Philadelphia was a scary place to us because it was so different than Jacksonville. There were always guys hanging out on the corners drinking, smoking, and sometimes singing. We would always cross the street every time we would come upon a group of guys since we didn't know if they would bother us or not. We didn't know anything about gangs at that age, but apparently these were very prevalent in Philly.

By the time I was in the sixth grade, we moved to an apartment with a common bathroom shared with some of the other tenants. I thought this was weird, but my mother became good friends with our neighbors and all the children got along so we just settled into the routine like everyone else. The apartment needed a lot of repairs though, especially the kitchen floor, which my sister fell through one day, injuring her leg. My mother was working by this time, and I will never forget how she would tell my sister and me what to wear to school each day and we often would change it once she left for work. One time, I was running for class treasurer of the student government and I had to give a speech. My mother laid out this rather ugly outfit for me to wear which consisted of a straight light blue skirt and a red pull over velvet sweater. I wanted to wear a pretty dress I had with beautiful colors and a velvet black stripe around the bottom and waist. It required one of those puffy slips so that it would stand out. I also wanted my hair in a nice smooth ponytail with the hair pinned under to create a bun. My brother was able to fix my hair exactly like I wanted it. I felt so proud going to school with a nice dress and my hair pulled up into that nice bun style. My teacher complimented me on how pretty I looked. I just smiled from ear to ear. I was not used to getting any compliments, so it made me feel really good. I wanted everyone to be proud of me and for our team to win the election. I got through my speech, finished the school day and arrived home in time to change clothes before my mother came home from work. Although disobedient, I looked very nice and ultimately won the election.

After sixth grade, we moved to Southwest Philadelphia into a brand-new low-income housing project, called Paschal Projects. Our house was three stories high and had four bedrooms, a living room, and an eat-in kitchen/dining room area. We were excited to have a new house to live in but unfortunately didn't have any food for several days after moving into this new house. We were probably the fourth or fifth family that moved into the complex due to our urgent need for housing at the time. By now my mother was suffering from diabetes and several other ailments and was considered disabled, which I'm sure moved us up the waiting list for one of those new houses. Up north in those days, there were several benefits available to women with a large number of children, which included welfare payments, food stamps, and assistance with furniture/clothing etc. I always hated the fact that we were on welfare. I felt so ashamed, and I'm sure others felt the same way. It irritates me when I hear those in power talk about people receiving benefits, such as food stamps and welfare, as if they are just lazy and want to take handouts. No. That is far from the truth. Circumstances and situations sometime drive families to seek assistance for a season and it shouldn't be considered the worst thing in the world to do. I remember being so embarrassed to fill out forms at school, which asked for your mother's place of employment and I had to enter N/A, with no mention of a father. This automatically let the teacher know that my family was on welfare. I also hated standing in line to get the free cheese and peanut butter the government passed out to poor people. When shopping at the store, using those food stamps, which came in different colors depending on their value, was just the worse. Poverty is a curse, and no one really wants to live in poverty. It crushes your self-esteem and causes you to feel as if you're somehow less than others because your family receives welfare benefits. Nevertheless, I was grateful that those benefits existed during that time or we would have gone hungry on many occasions.

Although my mother was set up to receive these welfare payments, due to our change of address, she somehow did not receive her welfare check when she was supposed to, and we ended up without food for more than a week. I recall eating cornbread every day for at least a week. We got creative with what we spread on top of it too. Such things as peanut butter, mustard, and catsup were just a few. After eating it for a week, I vowed not to ever eat it again, but it is now one of my favorite foods and if prepared right, it is a rather tasty food item. During that week when we had no money, we would search through some of the other houses in the process of being built to see if we could find something to sell to the local factory down the street. As I recall, we would take some of the floor tile which had not been laid yet and sell it to the foreman for change. I am sure he knew we should not have had access to anything like that since we were young kids. However, I was glad this man took advantage of his good fortune.

We earned enough to at least buy Kool-aide and some penny candy. We did not tell our mother, or we would have been in big trouble for sure. My mother was a very stern woman, and we knew she meant business when it came to us being obedient and doing the right thing. She was raised in the church, and she raised us in the church as well, so she was a strict disciplinarian. Her philosophy was that children should be seen and not heard, and no parents were trying to be your friend.

The year we moved to the projects was the year I met some wonderful friends that would remain dear to me for years to come. Elaine and Sharlene were their names. Elaine's mother was educated and well spoken. I believe she was a social worker. She had one son, Larry, and three daughters, one of which was very pretty, tall and thin and we just knew she would be a model one day. Elaine's mom was separated from her husband, who was the father of the youngest daughter (the pretty one) and she was trying to start a group home for the mentally retarded. She had acquired one patient at the time, a middle-aged lady, who was very quiet and somewhat strange. We were all scared of her only because she was different and not because she did anything to us. I do recall one day she picked up a dirty apple core to eat which someone had thrown on the ground and all the kids were laughing and pointing at her with disgust. I am sure Elaine and her sisters were very embarrassed, but they just took her back in the house and told their mom what she had done. After that, she didn't come out as much anymore but stayed in the house staring into space as I recall. Even then, I knew there was something wrong with making fun of people who were different due to no fault of their own. I knew I had compassion in my heart for this lady and people in general. However, in those days I wanted to go along with the crowd, even a small crowd to feel like I belonged.

Sharlene's family was a very large family of 12 children and everyone teased her about having so many brothers and sisters. It was interesting how different Sharlene's family was because her father also lived with the family, which was unique to us because most of the families were headed by single, divorced or separated women. The other unique things about her family was that the names of all 12 children began with the letters "Sh" and practically all of them stuttered. I remember playing games with my friends and the goal was to see who could name all the children in Sharlene's family. She was always so embarrassed by this and then she stuttered when she got angry, which didn't make her life any easier. I really liked her though and she was a good friend.

For some reason, in those days, everyone in the neighborhood liked our family even though there were only a few families living there at first. As the neighborhood grew, we became very popular because we were there first, and we had no glaring issues that people could identify, however, I knew differently.

My mom was very active in the community. She was instrumental in starting a girls' scout troop, of which my sister and I belonged, as well as a community organization to have a playground built in the neighborhood so the kids had somewhere to play. She also was the person everyone came to for advice if they had family issues or personal concerns. She was so good at what she did the Mayor set her up in her own office on Woodland Ave. to assist people with their mental health needs, much like a liaison between the community and the health care providers. She completed the initial assessment of what the person was dealing with and she would connect them to the appropriate agency. We were so proud of our mom since we were used to being on welfare and now our mom had a real job. My mom even worked well with the young men in our neighborhood and would try to steer them in the right direction. They all looked out for us as compensation for her listening ear and support.

I recall wanting to attend a party in the neighborhood with a friend, Cecelia, whom we called Ceil, and my mother was adamant that I could not go. When I told her that one of the real tough guys in the neighborhood, Michael whom she befriended, would be there, she said "Oh if Michael is going to be there then you can go." I was grateful for the relationship my mother had with our neighbors both young and old, as well as the status she held as a community activist. I believe a lot of my beliefs about giving back to the community are because of the work my mother performed during those years we lived in the Paschal Projects. I recall several of us blocking traffic on Woodland Avenue (a busy street in Philly) when there was a cause she was fighting for, such as use of the community center for after school programs and more security in the neighborhood due to increased crime. We also took bus trips to Washington DC to march with large groups of other people from other neighborhoods. It was a lot of fun and everyone was excited to be associated with fighting for a cause, any cause that would allow one to forget about their personal hardships and focus on those around them, for the good of all the people.

I believe God intended for people's lives to intertwine for common causes and to stand up against injustices. I still believe that today, but it seems like the church of today would rather remain quiet and continue to fill the church houses on Sundays and Wednesday nights and close their eyes to the injustices faced by communities all over this nation. I tell people all the time that I am so thankful Dr. Martin Luther King, Jr. didn't only concern himself with his family and church but put his life on the line to stand up for justice for the African American community. I admired him as one of the most important historical figures of our generation. So much so I insisted that my oldest son attend Morehouse College in Atlanta Georgia just like Dr. King, to possibly instill in him the same level of commitment to humanity.

As I noted, our family had a good reputation in the neighborhood because from the outside it appeared that we had no glaring issues, yet I knew differently. For me, although outside of the house I came across as a normal intelligent young girl, inside I lived in fear every day because of things my oldest brother would do to me. This is the same brother that hit me in the head with a brick when I was around two years old and threw our dead puppy into my arms when I was around four years old. For whatever reason, he appeared to be jealous of me. I was smart in school, but he was in the remedial classes; I was thin in those days and he was overweight. I don't know for sure if those were the reasons he seemed to hate me so much that he was always trying to hurt me but it's all I could come up with at the time. It did not explain the incidents that occurred at two and four years old.

Some of my memories of those years in the projects were filled with fear and dread each day my brother came home from school. I was always being hit and punched by him, cursed at and on several occasions held against the heater until my skin burned on my hands and thighs. I still have the scars to show for it. I was chased through the house with the threat of being stabbed until I would run and lock myself into the bathroom, but then one day he set the door on fire. Thank God my other brothers and sister were able to put the fire out without calling the fire department or me being burned. My stomach was always in knots for fear of what he was going to do. I often resented my mother for not protecting me from him, but most of the time she was not at home when he did these things. I often felt like she was afraid of him too. On one occasion, my mother purchased a cute little stereo system for my sister and me to play our records on but my brother, who always tried to "keep up with the Jones", was upset because it was not a large stereo system like our neighbor's across the street. So, what did he do? He took a hammer and demolished that cute little stereo, breaking it into little pieces. I don't think my mother had even paid for it in full yet. My sister and I just stood there and cried our eyes out. I literally hated my brother growing up and could not wait until he would move out of the house.

Although full of fear, I always worked hard to get good grades and kept the house clean. I was almost obsessive compulsive about it;

wanting everything to be perfect. What I could control, I controlled, because I knew I had no control over what my brother did to me. When I think back on it now as an adult, I believe the enemy used every tactic available to try to destroy who God wanted me to be by driving me to the place of walking in fear, which caused me to be more introverted, but also wanting to be accepted and loved. When someone hates you and you can't understand why, you begin to think that there must be something wrong with you and people will find out what it is so if you don't say anything, no one will know. That was some very stinking thinking and I am grateful that God later changed that narrative and I am stronger because of all that I went through and survived. I remember God saying to me that "the scars are just a reminder that life tried to kill you but couldn't." Oh, now that will make you shout, at least it made me shout at the time.

There was one place of solace for me during the years of fear and abuse, and that was church. I loved going to church. My mother raised us in church, but there were times that she didn't go or no one in the family wanted to go, so I would go by myself. I just loved being there. No one said anything to me and I didn't say anything to anyone else, but I would sit quietly and listen to the songs, the message by the minister and just feel safe for those few hours on Sunday. As I recall I was around twelve years old when I would walk to church alone on many Sundays and I just felt close to God somehow. I remember getting baptized at the age of 5 and I knew I had asked Jesus to come into my heart and be my Lord and Savior and really understood it to the extent I could at 5 years old, even though I always thought older than my age.

It was at Mt. Ararat Baptist Church in Jacksonville, FL, where I was baptized at the age of five by Reverend Dallas Graham. He was a well-loved Pastor, and Mt. Ararat was considered a very large church back in those days; now with the mega ministries that exists it would be considered a moderate sized church. I just loved going there and thought it was very pretty with its stained-glass windows and large round tubular shaped lights that hung down from very high ceilings. I guess at the age of five, however, everything looks larger. Mt. Ararat had several great choirs, of which my mother was the member of one, I believe it was choir 2B. They even had several usher boards for the large congregation. My Aunt Leola Morris was the president of one of the usher boards and my grandmother, Nellie Price, was a Deaconess. Although young, I enjoyed all the great singing, watching the choirs, ushers and deacon board's march into the sanctuary to music every Sunday. Everyone dressed up to go to church in those days, not like today where you can wear whatever you want to from jeans, shorts and t-shirts to suits. We always wore our best clothes and I liked to dress up in my lacy dresses and ribbons in my hair because it made me feel pretty. Both my sister and I had long thick hair back then and my mother, being a beautician (which is what they were called in those days) took pride in making sure our hair always looked nice. As we grew older, that long hair had to go. Silly girls we were, since some of our friends wished they had long hair.

Another major event happened when I was five years old. My grandmother, Nellie Price, passed away. My grandmother had long silky gray hair with very high cheekbones, like a Native American. She was very sickly and while living with us the ambulance would often back up to our front door to take her to the hospital. In those days, the ambulances looked like a funeral hearse, but only white. I used to dread seeing those cars. Apparently, she had a stroke at some point, which impacted her ability to walk without dragging her left leg when she walked. You could hear the sliding of her bedroom slipper against the floor as she walked down the hallway holding onto the wall for balance. It was rather scary that even after she died I could still hear her dragging that one leg down the hall. She often had a persistent cough and my mother would buy her Luden's cough drops to help. My sister and I would sneak into her room while she was asleep and take her cough drops because they tasted like candy to us. They came in a gold colored box with yellow cough drops or in a white box with red cherry cough drops. When she felt well enough, she would babysit us when my mother had to go out. As a young person, I was a "plunderer", always investigating things, trying to see what I could find to learn about. One such time, I was up in the medicine cabinet in the hallway bathroom taking the bottles down looking at them and putting them back, just plundering. Well, there was a bottle of ginger-violet, a purple medicine my mother used to paint one of my brother's tongue to relieve some type of issue he had. While looking at the pretty purple bottle, it slipped out of my hand and burst on the floor, spilling purple medicine all over the tile floor of the bathroom. My grandmother came in to see what happened, and she saw the big mess I had made and tried to help me clean it up. It was not coming up and I ran and got in the bed because I feared what my mother was going to do to me and rightfully so. My grandmother said, "no need for you to get in that bed, you know Lou Ellen (that was my mother's name) is going to get you when she comes home." Well, when my mother came home, my grandmother showed her what I did, and my mother snatched me out of that bed and beat me so bad with an extension cord that she drew blood. It's a good thing child abuse wasn't as widely discussed and monitored back then as it is today because my mother would have gone to jail for sure. I had so many bloody whelps all over my body that it took days for them to go down. From that day forward, I didn't "plunder" anymore, and after that, I started to be afraid of my mother. We loved our grandmother very much, because she always had a sweet disposition and spoke softly to us. My sister and I really liked that since my mother often yelled and had no problem using the rod of correction. My grandmother had been married to Matthew Price, who owned his own farm in Providence, Florida before they were run off it by white men in the middle of the night. He was also a minister of the Gospel, which causes me to be proud of our heritage of ministers of the Gospel. Unfortunately, he passed away when my mother was only two years old, so we never met him, but we loved our grandmother and cried uncontrollably when she passed away. My mother had said that whenever her mother passed, she was going to move back to Philadelphia. So, we did just that a few years later.

While growing up in the projects in Philadelphia, there was a great place where my friends and I had fun and that was the Elmwood Skating Rink. We spent many Friday, Saturday and Sunday evenings at that skating rink. The goal was to learn to skate backwards well, which took a lot of practice, but we mastered it and then had to show off our skills. The guys that skated at the rink were the best however and there was nothing better than to watch the all-male skate session. They were awesome to watch because not only did they skate well backwards, they could skate fast, as well as dance in unison. My girlfriends and I would dress alike in our Wrangler jeans and matching tops, which we purchased at the Lerner's Department Store on Susquehanna Avenue. We had to have our own skates and they had to have the multi-colored pom-poms on the toe with the bell in the center. The wheels on your skates had to be worn down just right to ensure you could make those corners and master those fancy steps when skating backwards. Oh, those were the days. One song that stood out to me from the rink was the song by the Dell's called Stay in My Corner. The DJ would call for couples only skate and it was a rather long song, so we were always nervous to see if anyone would asked us out to skate couples only skate. Sometimes we would be asked out and sometimes we wouldn't, but at the end of the day we were just glad to be there amid the crowd having a great time.

I enjoy thinking about the fun times I had growing up; although they were few, they were memorable. For some reason, however, I always felt older than my age and seemed to gravitate to older people over the years. I enjoyed listening to older people talk and discuss life, yet I did a lot of private thinking about life and its meaning and how I wanted mine to be different than what I was experiencing. I vowed not to have a lot of children or live in poverty and as I recall wanted to love and be loved but didn't think much about marriage. I initially wanted to be a career woman, to be somebody. Time would tell, but I knew I had to work hard in school, get good grades so that I could go to college and have a "good" life.

Birth of My Little Sister

While living in Paschal Projects, my mother reconnected with a married man that she had dated when we lived in North Philadelphia. I still didn't understand why she dated married men. Nevertheless, yet again she became pregnant by a married man. My younger sister was born on July 6, 1966. I remember it well since my mother had to go into the hospital a few days prior to her birth because she was diabetic and was having some complications. At that time, not everyone knew my mother was pregnant because she had a large girth due to her being obese. Even her own children did not know, although I could tell her abdomen looked larger than usual, but I just thought she was gaining more weight. Well surprise, surprise. My sister was born, and we were not prepared for another addition to the family, which now equaled seven children, but we welcomed her just the same.

We were very low on food during this time since my mother had spent several days in the hospital, but on July 4th, a miracle occurred, or at least I thought of it as a miracle. I was riding on the bus to visit my mother in the hospital, had no money and had not eaten because there wasn't anything at home to eat. When riding the bus or trolley, I would usually try to sit close to the front near the driver for safety purposes. Those seats weren't always available, but, on this day, there was a seat open right across from the driver. As I sat down, my eyes caught sight of something on the floor near the driver's seat and it appeared to be money. I looked closer and sure enough, it was a five-dollar bill. I stood up and looked around at the other passengers and it seemed like no one saw this money but me. So, I reached down, picked it up and asked the driver if it belonged to anyone. He said "no" as nonchalant as he could, and so I put that five-dollar bill in my pants pocket and thanked God that I saw it. I was able to buy a loaf of bread, some bologna, and a few packages of Kool-aide to make dinner for my brothers and sister. I was just as happy as a lark to have found that five-dollar bill. I believed with all my heart that God placed that money right there for me to receive because, He promised not to forsake the righteous nor cause His seed to beg for bread. My faith in God increased that day, even at the tender age of 11 years old.

After living in the projects for several years, my mother was able to finally move us to a nicer part of town, West Oak Lane. I was in the eleventh grade by then and did not want to change schools since I wanted to graduate with the classmates I had attended school with since junior high. I was a cheerleader and a straight A student and didn't want to start all over in a new school. In those days, the school system was not as strict about where you lived, so I had to take the trolley, the subway train and another bus to get to school every day. Before moving to West Oak Lane, we were able to walk to school, so now to take three different modes of transportation every morning and evening was a major adjustment.

I was very nervous about riding the subway for several reasons. One, I had never ridden it before, two, I didn't want to get lost because it traveled very fast and I wasn't sure I would be able to get off timely and thirdly because I heard it could be dangerous. All that being understood, I had to take my chances and I tackled my fears and rode the subway. It was scary and one of my fears was realized one evening on my way home when a man sat down next to me and exposed himself and began to masturbate right on the subway. Since I was sitting next to the window, I pushed my way out of the seat by knocking his legs towards the aisle as I got up and stood near the doors. I thought to myself, he is so gross. I wanted to vomit. That by far was my worse experience in riding the subway, but as time went by, I got used to riding it and settled in like everyone else.

We were proud to finally live in a house in a nice neighborhood. The house was previously owned by a dentist, with his office and exam rooms in the basement. My mother, younger sister, and one of my brothers made their bedrooms in the basement, while the rest of us had bedrooms on the second floor. My older sister, Myrtia, and I shared a room, two of my brothers (Ronald & Gregory) shared a room, and then my oldest brother, Linwood, had a room to himself.

Being new in a neighborhood can be very interesting. You often are met with mixed emotions by those who have lived there for a long period of time, especially girls. They don't like the fact that the boys in the neighborhood may be interested in you, a new kid on the block, when they have invested a lot of time and energy into building those relationships. It didn't help that our southern accent was still detectable, especially since we called our mother "Momma" while everyone up north called their mothers, Mommy. They would make fun of us for that and try to talk with a southern accent to tease and make fun of us. We tried to ignore them, but it always bothered us just the same. My sister and I always dressed neat and made sure our clothes were clean and ironed before going outside, even during the summer months. We would iron our shorts and tops and fixed our hair as if we were getting ready for school, even though we were only going outside to sit on the front or back steps. As time went by we got to know some of the kids in the neighborhood but never really was close with anyone. The boys used to tell us about their war stories when they were in the gangs. One even told us about when he was shot in the leg while running and didn't even know it until he looked down and saw the blood. There were several gangs in Philadelphia and it was always scary to me. Even though we moved to a nicer area of the city, there were still gangs around. We would always try to be in the house when it turned dark because you just never knew what would happen otherwise.

There was one young lady who lived across the street from us, whose mother looked more like her sister than her mother. The young lady was very heavy set and pleasant to talk to, however, her mother was slender and often dressed well below her age for appropriateness. She would wear what we called back then "hot pants" and "halter tops", but her daughter was always covered up from head to toe. I could tell there was some tension between them because of it. Nevertheless, we made acquaintances and would spend time over to her house on occasion. On one of those occasions the mother served my sister and I alcohol. It was our first-time drinking alcohol, so we got drunk and were not able to go home in that state. Her mother called our mother and asked if we could spend the night since she knew my mother would be very upset with her for giving us alcohol. So, we spent the night. The next morning, we were about to leave to go home and this guy from the neighborhood was out front saying that I better not come outside, or he would beat me up. I don't recall what I had done or what he thought I had done, but he was scary, and I was not about to go out there. I called my mother and told her what was going on and she was livid. My mother could be very tough when she wanted to be, especially when it came to men. She often spoke negatively of men to my sister and me, most likely because of her past experiences. So, she came outside and demanded to know what he was up to and called for me to come out of the house, daring him to lay a hand on me. He fussed a bit but ultimately didn't touch me with my mother being there. It was these types of interactions, along with the growing gang violence that later caused my mother to move back to Jacksonville in 1973 but leaving me in Philadelphia because by then I had started nursing school at the Hospital of University of PA, which I will talk more about later.

With all the twists and turns through the years of abuse, poverty, and low self-esteem, there was a time when I used to cut myself. It seemed like I had so much pain inside of me that if I could just make slits in my legs with a razor, some of the pain would ooze out. It was like a release, which really sounds so strange to me now, but I can remember the pressure I felt and the inability to vent or talk to anyone about what I was feeling. I'm not sure why certain things effect some people more than others even when they may go through some of the same experiences. All my brothers and my sister experienced the same lack as I did but although I was the only one physically abused by my brother, it appears I was always very serious about everything, wanting it to be different. I suppose I had an intensity about myself that they didn't have, and I always thought myself to be different from them, even adopted on some occasions. Sure, enough as I look back now, I am the only person among my siblings who graduated from college and did strive to have a better life than what we grew up knowing.

When I think back over those early years, I have mixed emotions, given the fact that all the things that occurred have worked together to cause me to be the person I am today, yet I think how my life may have turned out if I could have been spared some of those experiences. It is interesting how pain can impact purpose. The compassion I have today for service to others, the desire to see justice for all people, and the sheer drive to succeed all stem from those early years. The fear, inferiority complex, lack of self- love were the attributes of the fallow ground that God later broke by watering it with His precious Holy Spirit, changing my heart into a heart of flesh, and building my self-esteem through His Word. One scripture that literally transformed my life was Romans 5:8 personalized and repeated out loud about a hundred times; "But God commendeth His love towards Lynette, in that while Lynette was yet a sinner, Christ died for Lynette. This was good news since prior to that I saw myself pretty much as a group Christian, God loves us, God loves the Church, but it wasn't as personal as I knew God wanted it to be for me. It was life changing and the process continues.

High School Days

I graduated from high school at the age of 17 instead of 18, because I was one year ahead by starting first grade, instead of kindergarten, at the age of five years old. I really loved school and worked hard to be a model student with straight A's and an occasional B, a cheerleader, student government representative, national honor society member, make positive friends and liked by my teachers.

I attended John Bartram High School, home of the Bartram Braves. I often tell people my only claim to fame is that I graduated high school with Kobe Bryant's father, Joe Bryant, who was one of our basketball stars and for whom I cheered for as a cheerleader. Although sometimes quiet and introverted, I knew it was important to be involved with the right activities in high school, like the National Honor Society and Student Government, since it could impact my college acceptance. I practiced hard when I tried out for the cheerleading squad in 10th grade because I really wanted to be on the team, since it was a real stretch for my personality at the time. When I tried out, the team was made up of only white girls, even though our school was 60% white and 40% black. Therefore, being selected along with another friend of mine, who was also black, was a major accomplishment. By the time we made it to 12th grade, the team was all black, because the white girls started to drop off each year more black girls made the team. With an all-black squad, we moved away from those long skirts and sweaters they used to wear to a much shorter softer material skirt and turtleneck. Our school colors were burgundy and gray, so the skirts had alternating panels of burgundy and gray and the long sleeve turtleneck was burgundy. The outfit was cute, and we matched it with knee high burgundy socks, but we still wore those black and white tie up shoes. It worked well for the basketball season, but we froze our tails off during football season with the cold fall and freezing winters in Philadelphia.

It is sad how racism always raises its ugly head no matter how innocent or minor the situation or circumstances may be. During my 9th and 10th grade years, we still lived in Paschal Projects and we had to walk to school. There were no school buses for our neighborhood in those days. We lived several blocks away from the school, but it was still doable from a walking perspective. We were used to walking everywhere any way since our family didn't own a car. Unfortunately, there was this white man who lived on our route, who would open his door and command his big German shepherd dog to "sic" us. There was nowhere for us to run so we would jump on top of cars to avoid being bitten by this big dog. As previously mentioned, I was terrified of dogs, so this was a gut-wrenching fearful experience for me every time he did this. We hated walking past his house and would brace ourselves every day to be prepared to jump on a car when the time came. We never even considered that we may have damaged someone's car, but we didn't want to be attacked by the dog, so we did what we had to do and never even gave that a thought. We couldn't understand why he was doing this to us since we had never done anything even near his house and we didn't know him. One could understand somewhat if we had previously done something bad, like throw rocks at this house or something and he was trying to get back at us, but for us to know he only did it because of the color of our skin, which we could not change, it was difficult for our minds to comprehend. Thank God this all ended when we moved to West Oak Lane for my junior and senior years of high school. I then had to take a trolley, subway and bus to get to school each day. That was much better than having to run from a huge dog nearly every day.

Schools were integrated in those days, yet still internally segregated since all the white kids stayed together and all the black kids stayed together and there was not very much mixing of the two from a truly social perspective. There were the basic casual half-hearted greetings and we had some classes together, but no real genuine relationship building and friendships. Most of my teachers were okay and didn't demonstrate any blatant forms of racism that I can recall. I especially liked one of my white teachers, Mr. Salamone, who was Italian and taught 10th and 11th grade history. Everyone loved his funny nature and engaging teaching style, which included some smooth dance moves during his teaching sessions. Now to the other extreme was another white teacher who taught Trigonometry, but never engaged in conversations with the students at all. He basically wrote and explained math problems while facing the board during the entire class time. We rarely saw his face, only the back of his head. There was one turning point however, when he overheard a student talking about abortions, and he immediately stopped and yelled out "murder" while writing the word in capital letters on the board. We were all startled since he never spoke outside of the class material he wrote on the board. Everyone laughed even though it wasn't a funny subject but how he handled it sent the class into a frenzy of laughter. As students, we rarely thought of our teachers as people with lives outside of the classroom, but I realized differently when the husband or significant other was obviously abusing one of my gym teachers. She would come to school with bruises, and there were the rumors amongst the other teachers, as well as students and I remember just feeling so sorry for her, especially since she was such a pretty lady. I knew what abuse was like since I went through it myself with my brother but couldn't image what it would be like to have someone who is supposed to love you beat you up, giving you black eyes, as well as black & blue marks on your arms and legs. It was sad. I always vowed that I would never marry a man who would hit me.

Senior year was especially important since I knew it was the last year, and I would be starting my life as a college student the next fall. My biggest challenge was having all the money needed to cover the costs for everything like graduation pictures, cap & gown, prom, new clothes and all that comes with it. Well, since my mother was now on disability again, there were some things I had to do without such as new clothes. I had some basic things I wore, like my little black skirt with different color tops to make it look like several outfits. I pretty much wore different outfits each day but wore the same five outfits each week depending on the season of winter or spring. I loved my little black skirt. I was very thin in those days and loved wearing short skirts that fell mid-way on my thighs. I would get compliments from the other girls about the shape of my thighs although I thought I had horrible looking knees. I guess that's why I have trouble with my knees to this day because I spoke negative over them way back then. Learning to break the curse now. Nevertheless, my mother used to threaten to throw my little black skirt away if she saw it in the laundry, so I would wash it by hand to prevent that from happening. I so wanted to be considered attractive, even though in my heart I didn't think I measured up to the pretty girls in my classes. I think most teenage girls go through that phase but for me I would daydream about having nicer clothes and being prettier and would always envy the girls who dressed nice, came from a working two-parent home and was pretty, as well as popular. I think my popularity, although limited, was due to me being on the cheerleader squad and my committee activities. I had no problem giving a speech but wouldn't dare open my mouth in a group setting. I had too much of an inferiority complex, which I think stemmed from the poverty, physical abuse and low self-esteem. Those things can tend to silence one's voice, if you let it, which I did for a long time. Thank God, years later deliverance came once I found out who I was in Christ and how He loved me just the way I was but also loved me enough not to let me remain that way. My deliverance scripture was Romans 5:8 "But God commendeth His love towards us in that while we were yet sinners, Christ died for us." I made it personal by replacing "us" and "we" with "Lynette".

The Prom

I remember having a crush on a guy (nickname – Pockie) since 8th grade. He was on the baseball team and I knew his cousin very well because she lived down the street from my family when we lived in the projects. I let everyone know that I had a crush on this guy and it wasn't until the 12th grade did he give me the time of day. Many days it hurt because when I saw him on the street I would hope he'd speak, but no, he just kept walking and only gave me a slight glance. So, when he asked me to the prom, I thought it was a miracle. I was beyond excited and happy. My mother and I looked for the right dress and I got all dressed up and thought I looked as pretty as I could for this special night, only for him to pick me up so late that by the time we arrived at the prom, I didn't get my prom key (small replica of our school ring). We took pictures and danced a few dances and then it was onto the after-prom shenanigans. We met up with a group of classmates that I didn't know very well and unfortunately spent the rest of the evening with them. First, we went to the house of one of the girls to change clothes, at which time she made it very clear that she had feelings for the guy I was with. This group of girls would not typically be ones that I would consider or have as friends. They were really loud, and I considered a bit raunchy. After we changed clothes, we went to a restaurant to eat, only for those fools to run out without paying. I felt humiliated and very upset. I insisted that I would pay for my dinner, but they kept yelling for me to run or they would leave me. The evening did not go as I had planned. The girl that liked the guy I was with, kept making comments all evening to him about what she wanted to do to him and with me being rather shy at the time, I didn't open my mouth. However, the look of disgust remained on my face for the remainder of the evening. The big deal for after prom shenanigans was to go to Atlantic City and get hotel rooms, which we did do, but thank God the guy I was with did not try anything with me. He actually fell asleep. I was so glad, because I wasn't ready to be sexually active with him, and the entire evening was already a disaster from my perspective. It was sad because another guy, Greg, asked to take me to the prom also, but I turned him down to go with the love of my life, so I thought. It's funny how you make up all these fantasies in your mind about someone only to find out that they're nothing like you thought, UHHHH. To make matters worse, I found out the guy I turned down, took another young lady, and he rented a limo and made the night very special for her. I was thinking, darn that could have been me. Instead, I went with this fool and all his crazy friends.

The senior class trip was awesome, and I was so thankful that we were able to come up with the money for me to go since we were going to the Pocono Mountains. The snow was so beautiful, and we had a great time sledding down the mountain and not to mention the fun on the bus trip there and back. I was good friends with a guy (Rico) that was in several of my classes. He had transferred to our school to play on the basketball team, although he was short and didn't get a lot of playing time. Given we had Joe Bryant and a very strong starting five, I am not sure why he thought it was wise to transfer with the idea of playing. He was cute as a button, but I wasn't attracted to him in a girlfriend, boyfriend kind of way. In fact, that was the only real experience I ever had where I could say I was really friends with a guy and no thought of it being more than that. We hung out a lot on the senior class trip, along with some of my other girlfriends and had the best time.

Trip to Fort Lauderdale & The Big Decision

During the summer before my senior year, my neighbor, Mrs. Clark, came over to our house to introduce me to her nephew. I thought it was the older man that always tried to make passes at me and my sister when we would be sitting on the back steps when he visited. He disgusted us. So, when my mother called for me to come downstairs because Mrs. Clark wanted me to meet her nephew, I was so upset and took a long time to come down. Once I finally did, surprise. It was someone different, and he was very handsome. His name was Dennis. He was in his early to mid-twenties and I'm not sure why my mother was okay with me meeting him since I was only 16 at the time. We met and hit it off. He had his own car and he would take me out and we would hang out with his friends, all of whom were older than me. I thought I was in love. We had a favorite song by Al Green, "Let's Stay Together", which we would sing to each other when it came on the radio. I just loved his car. It was a supped-up Pontiac GTO. You couldn't tell me anything. I just knew I was grown. He even invited me to go with him to Ft. Lauderdale, Florida for two weeks and, believe it or not, my mother allowed me to go. As I understand it, he had told her that the doctor said he couldn't have kids, and Mrs. Clark, backed up the story, so off I went. It was my first time on an airplane and I was scared to death, but obviously survived. His family had a beautiful home and I had my own room and for the most part it was a pleasant trip, until one day a young lady shows up and says that she was from Philadelphia, and she was looking for him because she was pregnant by him. Well, I called my mother and told her, and she insisted that Dennis bring me back home right away. All the time he's reassuring me that it was not his baby, it couldn't be his baby, blah, blah, blah. My mother gave him a piece of her mind when we returned and again he reassured her that it was not his baby, and it was a girl that he had broken up with, and she wanted him back, but he didn't want to be with her anymore. That often happens when someone gets pregnant. By the time school started, we dated for a while longer and then a few months later we broke up too. By Thanksgiving, I too had missed my cycle for a few weeks, and I had to tell my mother that I thought I was pregnant. Well, sure enough, I was, and my mother made the arrangements and took me to the hospital to have an abortion. I didn't really think it was real, and I never actually considered that it was a baby. Sadly enough, I didn't have the courage to tell my mother no, I want to keep my baby and go through the shame and disgrace of being a teenage mother. My sister, however, also in the 12th grade, planned to get pregnant with her boyfriend, nicknamed Fish, and she made sure my mother knew she was going to have her baby and on March 29, my little niece was born. She wouldn't even let any of us touch her baby at first, and she was so proud of being a mom. I am so ashamed that I thought more of myself and my reputation than I did for the life I had inside of me and I was able to get through it by just thinking of it as a glob of tissue and nothing more. I don't recall if that is what the doctors told me or where I got that understanding, but that's how I rationalized it in my mind. I honestly don't think I have ever really grieved about what I did. I don't know if that's because my mother took me to have it done so it must have been okay, but, honestly, I think I might have tried to commit suicide if I did not have that abortion. All I knew is that I wanted to go to college and be a career woman, not have a baby at 17. This is not something I ever offer up in telling my story because of all the controversy around it, especially since I'm a Christian and was a Christian at the time I had it done, not to mention my mother was a Christian too. I'm sure if a poll was taken there are several people whose story is similar, but it doesn't make it right. According to the CDC, in 1971, there were 485,816 reported abortions performed in the United States and 586,760 performed in 1972. What's important to note about this is Roe vs. Wade, which legalized abortions wasn't passed by the Supreme Court until January 22, 1973, two years after I had my abortion procedure. I don't try to judge women today about this very sensitive issue knowing how I felt when I had it done, but I try to empathize with them and hope they would make a different choice, even though I wasn't able to do so. I always think perhaps the baby was a little girl, the little girl I never had. Looking back on the visit from the young lady while Dennis and I were in Ft. Lauderdale, she most likely was pregnant by Dennis, since it was obvious he had the capability to make a baby with me. After the abortion procedure, I was discharged home and ended up back in the emergency room two days later, because I was bleeding profusely. Apparently, they didn't do a complete evacuation, and I had to undergo a D & C (dilation and curettage) to stop the bleeding. If this happened to me, and I had my abortion procedure in a hospital, I can't image what happened to all the unreported abortions performed in those secret back rooms and alley ways. In some of these situations, women bleed so badly they must have a hysterectomy, which ends their ability to have children in the future. Thankfully, that wasn't my situation, although I did suffer a miscarriage after I got married and at that time really wanted to have a baby. I told myself it happened because of the abortion, and God was paying me back for what I had done. I later realized that God does not punish us for the mistakes we make, but natural consequences will sometimes appear to be payday for the deeds we have done. If we could pay the price for our sins then we wouldn't need Jesus, but because we could never pay our own sin debt, Jesus paid it all with His shed blood and I am so grateful for His forgiveness of sins, all my sins, even the abortion. I know one day I will see the precious baby I allowed to be aborted and I will need to seek her forgiveness, trusting that she will love me any way.

In June of 1972, I, along with one thousand and forty-five other students, graduated from John Bartram High School. My sister graduated from the high school designated for maternity students, but we still graduated the same year. Due to the size of my graduating class they did not call our names to receive our diplomas during our graduation ceremony. They only called out the names of the students who received scholarships and we obviously heard from our valedictorian and salutatorian. I applied for a nursing school scholarship through my guidance counselor and I had no idea if I had received it, but when I heard them call my name during graduation, I was so very happy because we needed every dime. Unfortunately, when I went to enroll into nursing school, I found out in fact I had not received it. I thought for sure I wouldn't be able to attend school but somehow the Lord made a way and I was able to enroll. My mother was very proud that both of her daughters graduated from high school. It was one of the happiest days of my life up to that point.

Nursing School

It was in December of my senior year when I received my acceptance letter from the Hospital of the University of PA School of Nursing, one of the most prestigious Ivy League schools in the nation. It was a three-year nursing program and then the fourth year would be completed at the university to obtain the Bachelor of Science degree in nursing. I was so excited and proud to have been accepted. In preparing to attend, I believe it was the most time I'd ever spent alone with my mother. We had to shop for the items on the list they mailed to us during the summer, which required three white uniforms and two pairs of those white nursing shoes. They required that I have two pairs, but my mother could only afford to buy me one pair. I was so scared that they were not going to let me enroll because I didn't have two pairs, but they never found out, thank God. Our head class leader was Ms. Hartung. She was a scary short petite lady with a squeaky voice and very mean. Once we started school, we had to dress in our uniforms, shoes and nursing cap and stand before her for approval and to pass inspection. She had to measure the length of our uniforms because it had to be so many inches below our knees. In those days they also had weight requirements for nursing students. Thankfully that was not a problem for me in my teen years since I weighed approximately 120 pounds and never worried about my weight back then. I passed inspection and was grateful that they didn't verify if I had the two pairs of shoes they required.

There were only seven black students in my nursing school class of over 100+ students. Our first year they assigned roommates and apparently, they made sure not to put us together; however, on the first day of moving into the dormitory, one of the white students caused a major scene when she found out that she would be rooming with a black student. She was screaming and crying, stomping up and down the hallway stating that she had never been around black people and she was not going to room with one. I felt so bad for her black roommate. There was a lot of tension amongst some of the students because of us black girls being a part of the class. I guess they didn't think we deserved to be there studying alongside of them, not realizing we had to work our butts off just to get accepted and then had to really shine in our classes. I vowed back then if I ever had children they would attend a good black college because I didn't want them to deal with what I saw and experienced in this predominately white school. Thankfully my roommate was cool. She was from New Jersey. As a matter of fact, she was too cool since she and her friends freely did drugs and she would sneak her boyfriend into our room to stay the night on several occasions, which made me feel uncomfortable and wasn't fair to me. We were not allowed to have boys beyond the "parlor" on the first floor, where we met with our guests, so for her to have this guy in our room overnight was a big deal to me but I never said a word.

We attended our nursing classes in the nursing school and all our science and elective courses we took at the University of PA. The grading system in our school was tough since a score of 80 = a letter grade of D. That was a shock because in high school a score of 80 = a letter grade of B. One therefore had to score a minimum of a

90 to get a B. It was tough, but I got through the first year with B's and C's which would have been A's and B's anywhere else.

The second year of school we could choose our roommates and I chose to room with a black girl, named Annette. We were good friends during our first year and did everything together, except smoke marijuana, initially, but more about that later. Since there was only seven of us, six of us stuck together, while one chose to spend more time with the white girls that allowed her to be with them, which was fine with us.

I experienced several new things in nursing school, specifically the freedom of being on my own to make decisions-within the restrictions of the school of course. We all were recipients of the Pell Grant and other grants due to the income level of our families. I sometimes envied some of the white students who bragged about the wealth of their families and how they got to travel home every weekend. There were two white girls from Miami Beach – Coral Gables area, who were cool with us black students, or at least they didn't act like we had the plague, and they traveled home every weekend unless we had a test on Monday. You could tell they were rich by their clothes and the fact that they always had money. My mother was able to secure me $32.00/month in food stamps, for which I was very grateful. We didn't have a typical cafeteria or anything, but we had a kitchen on each floor of the dorm and you could have a small refrigerator in your room, which I couldn't afford. Some of those girls were able to afford to eat out every night of the week or order in pizza and Chinese food, but we made sandwiches and often put on the longest skirt we could find so we could have a hot meal at the Father Divine's restaurant, which was across the street from our dormitory. You could get a hot meal for around $2.00 and the food was good, but you could not wear short skirts or sleeveless blouses. Thankfully, when we received our grant checks they were often more than we needed for school tuition and books, so we would have a few dollars left over to splurge a little. Otherwise, we were picking up snacks from WaWa's or dressing to meet the requirements to eat at Father Divine's, both across the street from our dormitory.

I tried to enjoy the social life on the campus of University of PA, which included parties, getting drunk and smoking marijuana (pot/weed/joint). I tried to drink to be social but did not like the taste of alcohol, which would remind me of my stepfather. I was always afraid that I may become an alcoholic as well. We would attend these parties where they would pass the joint around and everyone would take a puff, I would just let it pass me by. My roommate Annette enjoyed smoking marijuana and always would try to get me to smoke it with her and I usually refused until one day. We were in a park and she was smoking a joint and she kept after me to try it, so I succumbed to her constant nagging and took a few puffs. Well, I did not feel the same as when I drank alcohol and it caused me to feel spacey. Nevertheless, I smoked with her a few times after that as well. Several students in my school smoked it and even had those large pipes called bongs in their rooms. The one thing I noticed when I smoked I always saw someone whom I thought was one person but turned out to be someone else. I would walk up to someone and say hi and call a person's name only for them to say, I don't know you and that's not my name. I would be so embarrassed and quickly apologize for my mistake. I did not like that side effect of the drug at all.

A turning point came one night when I went out with this guy I had met, and he offered me a joint, and I smoked it with him and everything changed. We were in his car on our way back to my dormitory, and it appeared that every car was heading for us. I was so paranoid it was scary. When we arrived back at the dormitory we went into the parlor where I began to walk around the sofa in circles at a very fast pace. The guy I was with got scared and made a phone call to someone, and I was also very scared thinking, something must have been in that joint. It must have been laced with something else. Then the guy just left after making the phone call, so I was able to calm myself down enough to get to the elevator and go up to my dorm room. My roommate, Annette, had already left school (dropped out) by this time and I didn't have a roommate. When I was inside of my room I laid down on my bed to try to gather my consciousness because my head was spinning, and I was so worried that I may lose my mind. After a few moments, there appeared at the foot of my bed a glowing white figure, which I interpreted to be the Spirit of the Lord appearing to me. He called me by my name, "Lynette, you know you have been doing wrong. I am going to clean you up." When He said that immediately a blackness appeared at the foot of my bed as well and the white glowing figure and the blackness, which didn't have a frame but was misty looking, began to war at my feet. As the two were warring, which to me looked like they were warring for my soul, I had an out of body experience. I was hovering above looking down on my body, as if it were a dead body on a morgue table. Once the white figure won the warring session, there appeared like a white sheet that was placed over my feet and was pulled up until it covered my head, just like you cover a dead person in the morgue. Once the sheet covered my head, I immediately was back in my body and I was as sober as if I had never smoked that laced joint. I thought OMG, what just happened. I knew it was an encounter with the Lord. I figured my mother was praying for me, so the Holy Spirit intervened in my drugged-out state to rescue me. I am so grateful to God for that intervention because I always think about what could have happened that night. I could have lost my mind, or it could have led me to being strung out on some corner somewhere.

The next morning, I immediately called my girlfriend Annette, since we stayed in touch with each other and I told her what happened. She was shocked and then asked me to come to church with her the following Sunday. I quickly agreed and met her at her church that Sunday morning. I had never attended this church before and it was rather large, but we sat approximately three fourths of the way back from the front of the church. There were speakers up in the corner of these pillar type structures along the walls of the church. As the minister began to preach, he said "There's a young lady in the audience who needs to come back to God". As he was saying this his voice seemed to get louder and louder through the speakers and I just knew he was speaking to me. Keep in mind I had not been to church in a while since I had started college and had never attended this church, so the minister didn't know anything about me, but I just knew he was talking to me. I jumped up out of my seat and began to scream "Thank you Jesus, thank you Jesus" several times and my feet were moving in place very fast. After a few moments, I stopped and sat down. Totally shocked because I had never ever "shouted" in church. In fact, I was very reserved and wouldn't ever speak out in a congregation, especially this large. I asked my friend Annette, "was that me?" She said yes, and your feet were going a mile a minute. That was the beginning of my real spiritual journey. From that day to this, I have never touched another marijuana joint or taken a sip of any alcohol. I committed myself to living a Christian life and felt that I owed God since he rescued me from that drugged stupor I had found myself in a few nights before.

52

My first assignment as I saw it was to find a Bible Study to attend so I asked around and started to attend one recommended to me by a friend. When I joined they were studying the book of Revelations and the end times. It was so intense and compelling, I felt like I needed to be about my Father's business. I didn't have time for nursing school. The Lord was soon to return. I therefore did not invest much effort in my next course and sure enough because of that I didn't pass the class. I called my mother, who by now had moved back to Jacksonville, Florida to get away from Philadelphia and all its crime and gangs. She told me to come on home and that's all I needed to hear. When I think back on it, I so wished she could have talked me into taking the class again, which I could have done, and remaining in school, but that wasn't to be. The major ironic thing about me leaving school half way through my program was that I had aborted my baby with the reasoning of wanting to attend nursing school and here I was dropping out without even finishing. My mother sent me the funds to get the bus to Jacksonville and I signed myself out of school with the thought that I needed to start a new life in Jacksonville and serve the Lord since He was soon to return, or so I thought.

Experiences of Racism

When my brother, Ronald, was three years old, we walked to the store at the corner of Cleveland and Moncrief Rd. to get something for my mother. I was six and my sister was seven years old. Standing in the store was a white man, who did not like the fact that we entered the store and he told us to leave. He wasn't the owner of the store as I recall, just a man standing in the store. When we didn't leave, he flicked his cigarette ashes into my brother's eye. Oh, My Goodness. My brother screamed, because I'm sure it burned something awful. We then ran home to tell my mother what happened, and she ended up having to take him to the hospital. They treated him and placed a white patch over his eye. We all felt so bad and just could not understand why this man did that to my brother. I don't recall if my mother went to the store to address what happened, but it could very well have been because it would cause more problems if she did.

Growing up in a black neighborhood, you didn't experience racism if you stayed within your community, but who could do that? One always had to go to the store, the doctor or hospital, school and other places of business. I can't cover all the incidents that happened over my lifetime but will highlight those which impacted me the most.

I already mentioned the incidents in Philadelphia when my

sister and I walked to school along with our friends and this white man, who lived on our route tried to have his dog attack us, causing us to jump on the top of cars to avoid being bitten.

Another major incident that stands out in my mind is in 1978 when I worked for an insurance company in Charleston, SC. It was my first job in Charleston since we had moved there the year before right after the birth of my oldest son. I was the only black person in the office and I worked hard, minded my business and knew I was there to get a job done. I noticed however that all the staff members in the office were asked to relieve the receptionist for her breaks, everyone except me. One day, one of the staff members seemed irritated that she had to cover the front desk interrupting her work. So, I went to talk to my office manager about it, especially since I sat near the front desk. I inquired with her as to why I was never asked to relieve the receptionist and she in turn asked me to close the door and sit down, which I did. She began to explain to me that the general agent, Mr. Zervos, did not want a black person behind the desk when his clients arrived in the office to see him. At first, I was sort of shocked and said, "Oh Really"? Then, I just said "okay". When I walked out of her office, I had a choice to make, I could either make a big issue out of it, filing a discrimination suit or I could choose to learn everything in that office and perhaps one day run the place. I chose the latter. I learned every job in the office and years later I was promoted to assistant office manager and then the office manager took very ill and actually passed away, after which I was promoted to Office Manager. So, the moral of that story was I chose to take the high road and it paid off in a way that I didn't need to relieve the receptionist, but I was the person who now hired the receptionist. I knew in the early years, that to make a name for myself in this small town would not serve me well. I worked for that company 12 years, until they did a reorganization and eliminated all the field staff. Everything happens for a reason and so with the ending of this job, I chose to go back to nursing school and get my RN degree.

I decided to take all the pre-requisite courses prior to my nursing courses so that I could focus on my clinical training and nursing courses when I started nursing school. I did just that and completed them all with a 3.9 GPA. I sat for the nursing entrance exam and passed it receiving a score higher than needed to get into the nursing program. The next step was to apply, which I did. I then patiently waited for my acceptance letter. The day finally came when I received a letter in the mail and to my surprise, it said they were sorry to inform me that I was not selected to be admitted to the school for the fall semester. I said to myself, "this just can't be true". I received the letter on a Saturday and planned to be at the school first thing Monday morning to inquire as to why I was not selected to be admitted, based on my GPA and test results. When I arrived, I asked to meet with the dean, who kept me waiting for some time, but I was not leaving until I had some answers. When she finally met with me, I inquired as to the criteria used to select the students that were accepted into the program. She tried to explain herself and stumbled over herself repeatedly, which let me know she wasn't being truthful. I finally said to her well I'm not leaving this building until you can prove to me that the students you chose have a record more stellar than mine, otherwise you've discriminated against me. She then had the audacity to suggest that I go to school to be an LPN, which sent me over the edge because she knew a lot of black students chose to be LPNs rather than RNs. I politely said to her "I don't want to be an LPN, I plan to be an RN, and I plan to enroll in the program starting this fall unless you can show me how every single student you selected has a more stellar record than mine." At that, she suggested I meet with the acting head of the Health Science department. I let her know I would be glad to meet with him, but I wanted to meet with him that day. I waited a good while longer and finally got to speak with the acting head of the department. He was a very nice man, and I explained to him my situation; he said, "I am a believer, and I want to make sure everyone is treated fairly, so please let me investigate this and pull your records and you will hear back from me within two weeks." I said, "Sir, I am a believer also, so I know with the two of us, God will surely work this out. Sure, enough within the two-week time frame, I received a letter stating that a space has become available for me in the program for the fall semester. I did very well in nursing school, achieving a 3.51 GPA, which is somewhat rare for nursing school. I also was awarded the Merit Scholar Award, inducted into the Nursing Honor Society and gave the student address at graduation. During our reception after the nursing graduation, I was able to see the dean with whom I spoke with and who suggested I go be an LPN, and I said to her, "I'm so glad that I didn't go be an LPN since I did rather well in becoming a RN". All she could do was smile and say congratulations. A few years later, the President of the college invited me to sit on the advisory board of the school, which I did for two years. It's so important for us to understand that we don't have to accept every "no". There are times when we must fight for our rights to a certain education, job or position. I could do that because I knew I had the credentials to back up my position, which they could not deny. I also believe God places the right people in our lives at the right time to act on our behalf. So, the acting head of the department was in position to make it happen for me when the dean didn't appear to want to budge one iota.

Several months ago, I went to see the movie, "12 Years a Slave", which is not my typical movie to see since its so difficult to watch blacks being treated worse than animals; this movie didn't disappoint. When I looked around the theater, I saw several white couples watching it just as I was. I always wondered what they thought when they watched movies like this but never had the nerve to ask one of them. At the end of the movie, on our way out of the theater, I did find the courage to stop an older gentleman and his wife and ask that very question, I said "Sir, excuse me, but what do you think when you watch a movie like that"? By now, tears were rolling down my face because of the brutality seen in this movie and how painful it was to watch. He answered me and said he didn't understand how people could treat other people like that. I said to him I wish he could see how we really feel as black people being treated badly, because of the color of our skin, which we can't change. By now, tears are really rolling down my face, and he also started to cry and put his arms around me, without really saying anything, but I knew what he was trying to communicate. It was one of the most meaningful interactions I've ever had with a white person. It let me know that there are still people with a heart of compassion for others and all are not in agreement with the black stereotypical views many whites hold.

As a black person, when I meet a white person, I never think about whether I like them as a white person, but my mind always questions whether they may like me as a black person, not because of my personality but only because of the color of my skin. I have met and have grown to love several dear white friends, which has never been a problem for me and I think most blacks feel this way. We tend to be more open to interacting with whites than they are to interact with us, which is sad because they often miss out on opportunities to get to know some wonderful people and develop lasting relationships. I am thankful for the ones who are open to fostering relationships and consider our personal character rather than all the racist stereotypes, especially, Donna, who was led by the Lord to stop me from committing suicide several years ago. However, still to this day in 2018, we as black people continue to face incidents of racism and I can't say that it will ever be abolished in these United States of America but personally I will continue to take a stand against racial injustices which I and others may encounter. At the end of the day I believe wholeheartedly it's better to die for a cause if that's the result of taking a stand, than to live in agreement with blatant racism and injustice.

My First Marriage

In December of 1973, I moved back to Jacksonville Florida after leaving nursing school to pursue the work of the Lord, or so I thought. I moved in with my mother, because I was only 18 years old, turning 19 the next February. I quickly began to look for a job and was fortunate enough to land one at Blue Cross Blue Shield of Florida as a Claims Review Analyst. It required knowledge of medical terminology and since I had completed several courses in nursing, I was able to ace the test and began a three-month training program in January of 1974. I was very grateful for the job, although it didn't pay much, but, with overtime, I was able to earn a decent wage.

Now that I had secured my first job, I began to settle down in Jacksonville and, being a single young lady, I desperately wanted to meet a nice guy. One day, I took my little sister shopping at the Gateway shopping center and as we were standing waiting for the bus to return home, my eyes spotted this guy in a beautiful brand-new burgundy and white Pontiac Grand Prix. I said to myself, "now that's the kind of guy I would like to meet." Growing up, I always said when I get married, my husband will have a good job, drive a nice car and wear nice clothes. So far, this guy seemed to meet the external criteria. He then turned into the parking lot of the shopping center and my eyes just followed him. He drove over to a portable post office machine to purchase stamps, or at least that's what it looked like to me. He then drove back in the direction of where my sister and I were waiting for the bus. He stopped and asked me if I was a student at Bethune Cookman College, a college in Daytona Beach. I quickly responded "No." He then said, "Can I ask you something?", and I proceeded to walk over to his car to see what he wanted and somehow my right foot turned over due to either the pavement being uneven, or I was too anxious to get over there and tripped over myself. He asked me if I needed a ride somewhere and I told him I had my little sister with me and he said, "that's fine." My little sister overheard us and quickly said as loud as she could "I'm not getting in the car with no stranger. Momma said don't ride with strangers." I was a bit upset with her, but she was right, however, I wanted to meet this guy. He was dressed in burgundy and white to match the car and he was rather handsome with long sideburns. So, I told him never mind and it would be better for me to just wait for the bus. So, he asked for my phone number, which I gave him. I don't think I was home thirty minutes before he called and asked if he could see me that night. I responded with a big "sure." I must say, at the time, I wasn't too bad looking myself with my big Angela Davis afro and slender frame of approximately a size 9/10. In those days, I didn't worry as much about my weight unless my pants started to get tighter, which I did not like. Most girls liked wearing tight clothes, but I did not. I had to have a lot of slack in my pants, which were often high waist bell-bottoms in several different colors with matching pull over tops. I prided myself in dressing neat and keeping my afro tight with every hair in place. Therefore, even though I was anxious to meet him, he was anxious to meet me as well.

He came over that night, and it was the start of our relationship, which resulted in me later moving in with him approximately nine months later. I had moved out of my mother's house prior to moving in with him, because the State threatened to reduce her welfare check due to me working and living in the same house. I moved into this dormitory type facility downtown for single young ladies and I had a roommate who was very shy and quiet, so I often spent the night with my new boyfriend. We both agreed that it didn't make sense for me to continue to pay money for the room when I rarely stayed there. Now, shacking up with someone was not high on my list of things I should be doing but often when you're involved in sin you dismiss it as no big deal. I still went to church every Sunday and knew the importance of pleasing God with my actions and behavior. I just shoved the guilt into the back of my mind and carried on with my life, which I thought was better than it had ever been. My boyfriend had his own house, next door to his mother and father on the Eastside of Jacksonville. He had a good job working for Texaco Oil Company, he dressed nice and had two cars, one the new Grand Prix and the other he called his work car which he drove to work every day. We would take weekend trips to Daytona Beach and did a lot of riding around on the weekends to help me get more familiar with Jacksonville. He was nine years older than me, so I felt like I had found the right man. Because I was such a broken person during that season in my life, I don't know that I even knew what real love was but had fantasies in my head of what I thought it should be. Unfortunately, there was a gaping hole in my soul and I was expecting this man to fill it, not understanding at the time that no one can fill the hole in my soul but God. Nevertheless, I went through seasons of feeling like I was in love and then there were seasons of altercations because of our insecurities and inability to love unconditionally. We were both committed however to make it work, no matter what, or so we thought. I felt like I was hanging on for dear life, needing to be loved but never seeming to have that need met to my twisted expectations. I really needed to love myself first, which I did not, before I could fully give and receive true love.

God made this real to me years later.

So, after dating and living together over an eleven-month period, at the age of 19, I married my first husband, Rudolph L. Joyce, age 28 on December 20th, 1974 at the Duval County Courthouse. In my heart, I was thankful that I was no longer living in sin; now I was a married woman, which I felt would please God. We had our share of ups and downs, arguments and scuffles, but hung in there to make the relationship work for a total of 22 years.

Within a few months of being married, we were able to purchase a brand-new home located on Moncrief Rd. near Soutel Dr. We were so proud of our new house and we set out to decorate it nicely and start our new life together. The mortgage, as I recall was only $250.00 per month but to some people in those days it was considered a lot, but we were able to manage with both of us working with no children at that time. I didn't have any bills myself at first except to pay for the Tupperware and Avon I was always ordering from co-workers and friends. My husband took care of all the bills back then and I would buy groceries and the newest 45 record or album out from Motown because I loved to listen to music and dance. I was even able to purchase my first car, which was a brown Ford Pinto, that I had to later take back because I'd bit off more than I could chew financially. Thankfully, it wasn't too long after that my husband bought me a gray and black Toyota Corolla. I just loved that car, due to its size and the fact that it was brand new. I was not allowed to drive his Grand Prix, which should have spoken volumes, but I was just glad to have what appeared to be a good life and I was grateful. Then things began to change.

It was after our second Christmas together as a married couple, I experienced one of those turning points in our relationship, and I honestly can't fully explain why it had the impact it had on me, but it just did.

I wanted to surprise my husband with a very nice watch for Christmas, a Bulova, which was very expensive back then. I put it on lay away, and every payday, I would drive over to Regency Square Mall and make a payment on this $500.00 watch. I was so proud to be able to give this watch, because I had never really purchased things for my boyfriends in the past, because I never had a job and didn't have the money to buy gifts for friends or anyone else for that matter. It took me weeks to pay off this watch, but, when I did, I had the biggest smile on my face walking out of that jewelry store with the bag in my hand. I wrapped it all pretty and placed it under the Christmas tree to await his expression on Christmas morning. Well Christmas morning came, and I was so eager for him to open my special gift. He opened it, and he didn't have the response that I was expecting; he said it was nice and thanked me for getting it for him. I felt like someone had just let the air out of my happiness balloon, although this wasn't the worse of the impact of my gift, for it was what happened a few days later that shifted my heart in a way I wasn't expecting.

My husband was a big sports fan, and you would often find him in front of the television watching all types of sports from football, basketball, baseball, boxing, track & field or tennis. It didn't matter what it was, but he would usually be watching it. I walked in the door from work this one afternoon a few days after Christmas to find a brand-new color TV in the living room. It was a unique looking television like something from the Jetson since it was a one-piece white curved floor model TV with a pedestal bottom. So, I asked my husband where he got the TV from, and he told me that he took the watch back that I had bought him for Christmas and purchased the TV instead. Oh, my goodness, I was not expecting this at all. My heart just sank to the floor as I thought about all the weekly trips I made to the mall to pay on that watch and how proud I was to give it to him since it was the nicest gift I had ever given anyone, and I just started to cry. This one act hurt me so bad at the time that I could not get over it and I honestly didn't feel the same about my husband from that day forward. Again, I don't fully understand why it had such an impact on me, but it did, and it was the first turning point in our relationship.

After that incident, it seemed like arguments were more intense and I displayed much more anger during those altercations. I didn't have the same desire to walk on egg shells to ensure I didn't do anything to jeopardize this so-called nice lifestyle we created. There were a few bruises experienced that I explained away but another turning point came when my husband chased me out of the house with his gun. That was a scary situation and I drove home to my mother's house for consoling, staying away for a few days. I was not willing to go back to living with my mother, or trying to find something I could afford, which I knew wouldn't be much. Thankfully, my husband apologized, I went back home, and life went on as usual.

A few months later, I missed my cycle and a pregnancy test indicated that I was pregnant. This would be my second pregnancy and now that I was married, my husband and I were very excited about the news. I planned to have this baby and I would not even think of ever having another abortion. So, I selected an OBGYN physician, who unfortunately had a weird name, Dr. Finger, to be my doctor. I had my first appointment and he confirmed that I was indeed pregnant, and we went through the preliminary preparation of taking prenatal vitamins and ensuring that I was eating more nutritious food than a lot of the junk food I had been eating but still not gaining a lot of weight. Two months into the pregnancy, I woke up one morning and realized that I was spotting. I called my doctor and he just told me to put my feet up and stay on bed rest until my regular appointment the following week. Since this was my first full pregnancy experience, I didn't know that he really should have examined me instead of blowing me off for another week. I did what he said and went into the office the following week for my usual appointment. I told him I didn't feel the same, so he decided to exam me and after doing so, he yells at me saying "You loss tissue." You're no longer pregnant, you loss tissue." I am in tears by now because I'm in shock that I was no longer pregnant and the way he was speaking to me was just awful. It was the worse bed side manner I had ever seen. I had miscarried my baby and this doctor was not comforting at all. So, I gathered myself, got dressed and left to go home. I called my husband and my mother to tell them the terrible news. My mother was asking a lot of questions about whether I needed to have a Dilation & Curettage (D&C) or if he had done an ultrasound, my answer to both was no. She then had me questioning whether I had loss the baby since he didn't do an ultrasound or determine if I had discharged all of baby's remains. My husband was upset as well and tried to comfort me the best he could. I even felt worse because he already had one son and now I felt inadequate because I miscarried our first baby together. Thoughts also flooded my mind that this was pay back for me having the abortion when I was 16 years old. A part of me felt like I had paid my penance for that awful sin and now a life for a life, so we're even God. This was indeed stinking thinking, but this is what I thought at the time.

The next day I found another doctor, made an appointment for that day and sought a pelvic examination and confirmation of either pregnancy or miscarriage. The new doctor did confirm that

I had a miscarriage, and I didn't need a D & C. I sunk into a state of depression for several months after this, blaming myself for the miscarriage because of the abortion. It wasn't until I missed my cycle again for a couple of months that I began to think I would experience joy again. Sure enough, I was again pregnant for the third time. This pregnancy, however, felt different. I was sick every morning and didn't mind it because it confirmed that I was pregnant, and I was going to have a baby. I waited to tell anyone until I was beyond the first trimester. Once I got past that time frame, I began to feel a little more confident that I was going to be a mother. We would have a family, and all would be right with the world.

During my pregnancy, my husband found out that his job was relocating to Charleston SC and we would need to relocate there, or he would need to find another job. Well he had been with Texaco for several years and it was a good job with good pay and benefits. In addition, with me being pregnant, it was not the time to change jobs, so we decided that he would relocate to Charleston in June of 1977 and I would remain in Jacksonville until after I gave birth to the baby, which was due in August. That's what we did.

My husband rented a small one-bedroom apartment in Charleston and would drive home every weekend so that he would be home with me as much as possible during the pregnancy. I continued to work at Blue Cross Blue Shield until the start of my maternity leave and pending relocation.

On the afternoon of August 10, 1977, at approximately 5:19 p.m. I gave birth to my first son, Derrick Donnell Joyce, at Baptist Hospital downtown Jacksonville, weighing in at 8lbs. 10 ounces, which matched his birthdate. It was the happiest day of my life. Because my husband worked the second shift (3:00 p.m. – 11:00 p.m.) and did not have a home phone or cell phone back then, I had to wait until he arrived to work at 3:00 p.m. to let him know I was in labor and that it was likely I would deliver that day. Since Charleston SC is approximately four hours from Jacksonville, he left immediately after my call around 3:15 p.m. but did not arrive in time for the birth, which occurred two hours later. Unfortunately, I was alone at the hospital to give birth to my first son. Although I went to Lamaze classes in preparation for natural childbirth, I ended up getting the drug Scopolamine and was out cold during the delivery. I woke up to a nurse kneading my abdomen to help discharge the afterbirth, which was painful. I remember grabbing her arm, asking her to stop; she jerked away stating she had to do it or I would have major problems. So, I endured the pain and looked forward to seeing my baby.

My bottom hurt so badly, because I had to have an episiotomy due to the birth of an eight-pound ten-ounce boy. It felt like they had ripped open every muscle that existed in the area, causing me to walk on my tiptoes, unable to place my heels on the floor. One awesome thing about childbirth, however, is once you hold your baby, the memory of all the pain is not as important because of the joy of bringing a life into the world.

My husband finally arrived at the hospital and was able to see his second son (he already had one son from a previous relationship) and be there to assist me during my hospital stay. Once discharged home, I found myself quite nervous about managing the care of a new baby, nursing my childbirth wounds, and preparing to relocate to Charleston SC. We never know just how strong we are until we are put to the test and survive, doing what we must do for the season at hand.

So, in October 1977 we rented our house to my cousin, Diane and her husband, and then relocated to North Charleston SC, where we rented a town home in the Pepperhill subdivision. Since we were used to owning our own home but was not familiar enough with the area, we stayed in the townhouse until the end of the lease and then purchased a doublewide mobile home. It was the first time I had lived in a mobile home and realized that they were quite nice and spacious. We had four bedrooms, a family room, a living room, a dining room, and a kitchen. We rented a space in a mobile home park off Dorchester Rd, in North Charleston and began our lives with our son, who was about 8 – 9 months old by that time. I was grateful not to be working and trying to take care of a baby, especially since he would not sleep through the night. The challenge for me, however, was that my husband only gave me $5.00 spending money every two weeks when he got paid. Yes, you read it right, FIVE Dollars. One thing about my first husband, he was very frugal and tight with his money. He took care of the house and everything, but what could I buy with $5.00, even in 1978. This led me to want to get a job so that I could have my own money and purchase the things I wanted to, such as my toiletry items and an occasional outfit.

I applied to several temporary agencies, and I was called in for an interview with Snelling & Snelling. They scheduled me to interview with Mass Mutual Life Insurance Company in downtown Charleston on the corner of King & Queen Street. They advised me that I would need to take a typing test, which concerned me because I had not typed since high school. Although I graduated with a College Preparatory degree in the top 10% of my class, I dropped French my senior year and took typing instead so that I would know how to type. The other issue was I didn't have access to a type writer either, therefore, I went to the library to practice typing so I would be ready to past the typing test. It paid off because I aced the test, the interview went very well, and I was hired as a correspondence clerk. So, when my son Derrick was one year old, I started working and was so very excited to have my own money to spend. I was the only black person hired in the office and this is the same company I mentioned earlier where I was not able to relieve the receptionist because the general agent didn't want his clients to see a black person behind the desk when they entered the office. I worked hard and was eventually promoted to the office manager and was able to hire the receptionists so that incident was a catalyst for me to excel and prove to them that as a black person I had a right to be there because I was smart, and they needed my expertise and knowledge. I was a quick study and learned every job in the office, which included managing new business applications, correspondence, death claims, double entry bookkeeping and system's administrator of the Wang computer system we used. I worked for that company 12 years and really enjoyed the work. It was a small office of administrative staff and several insurance agents. We had a lot of fun and everyone got along rather well, except for the older lady I was assigned to work with when I first started. She had been with the company for 25 years and she didn't let you forget it. She transferred to Charleston from the Syracuse office due to her husband's health. I was to receive my daily assignment from her after we went through the mail. Well, she took most of the morning just to go through it, which drove me nuts. There was such a backlog of correspondence that needed attention, but she spent so much time talking she couldn't focus on what she was supposed to be doing. Relief came when she took a three-week vacation and I had to manage the workload on my own. There were stacks and stacks of mail backlogged but I focused and made sure I had everything caught up to date by the time she returned. You would have thought she would have been pleased but, oh no. She was very upset and upon her return stormed over to my desk and said, "Who do you think you are trying to show me up? "I've got 25 years under my belt and you think you can just come in here and try to show me up?" I said, "Listen Helen, which was her name, I'm here to do a job and I did it so you need to just get out of my face." My office manager heard us going at it and called us into her office. I explained the situation and she asked for any suggestions on how we should manage the work going forward, to which I suggested that we split the alphabet for assignment of the incoming correspondence and that Helen could choose which part of the alphabet she wanted, and I would take the remainder. It was easier for me to work by myself and get the work done because I could not stand all that talking and dragging out the workday, which I'm sure is why she was in a backlog when I got hired. My manager agreed, and from that point on, I did my work, minded my business, and made sure I listened as intently as possible to learn the other work in the office. I often volunteered to cover the other girl's desk when they were out, so I could learn their jobs. This paid off, and I always recommend to my mentees to make it a point to learn as much as possible about what others are doing in your work place because the more you know the more valuable you are to the organization.

Well we lived in the mobile home for another year and a half before purchasing a four-bedroom brick single family home in the Forrest Hills subdivision, also off Dorchester Rd. My husband still lives in that home to this day, which has been paid off now for several years. A lot of growth took place while living in that home and I can recall the happy times as well as the times when I was so depressed and sad I would curl up into a fetal position and cry my eyes out, not being able to manage my emotional pain. I was so hungry for the demonstration of love to be extended by my husband, but not understanding that he couldn't fill that void in my heart because I didn't even love myself. There were days I just wanted to die, but then there were other days when there was a glimpse of joy. My husband was not an affectionate person and would rather sit and watch television than communicate or snuggle up on the sofa. He was old school in that he felt I should have been happy with him working, providing for the family and taking us on our twice a year vacations to either Myrtle Beach SC or Orlando Florida where we owned a timeshare in the Windy Hill Resort and Vistana Resort near Disney World. I seemed to always be so uptight I could barely enjoy the vacations fully but was always excited to go for a change in scenery. I made the best of the times and enjoyed being there.

Death of My Younger Brother

In September 1980, my second youngest brother, Gregory, at the age of 21, committed suicide at home with a hand gun while sitting on the side of the bed in a bedroom he shared with my youngest brother, Donald. It was the same house my husband and I had purchased and was renting to my mother, after my cousin and her husband moved out. I'll never forget receiving the call from my mother on Friday, September 13 that he had shot himself, and I wasn't clear at first if he was dead or not. Once I understood he was, in fact, deceased, I made plans to travel from Charleston to Jacksonville to be with my mother and family during this horrible time. I packed clothes for Derrick and myself and left first thing that Saturday morning. My husband was not able to leave with us due to work but would attend the services as soon as we had made arrangements.

My brother had been troubled for several months leading up to the incident after someone had placed PCP in his drink at a party one night. It caused him to be very paranoid and unable to manage life effectively. I guess he was tired of dealing with it and decided to take his own life. Unfortunately, my brother Donald was in the same dark room when my brother Gregory pulled the trigger. He said he heard a loud pop, saw a flash of light from the gun and he then jumped up and ran out of the room. Since my brother shot himself in the head, the walls were splattered with brain matter and blood. The ambulance was called, and he was pronounced dead on the scene. According to my mother, it was so difficult for her to see her child being carried out of the house already deceased. Since I didn't arrive until the next day, I had to rely on the details being reported by others. The city did send a clean-up team to wipe down the walls and clean the room of any evidence of what had occurred, which was indeed a blessing; I don't know that any of us in the family would have been able to do it. After the clean-up, we kept the door closed. My mother knew that wasn't the thing to do or we many never go into that room again, so she opened it, and we all went in there together for the first time after the incident. Although my brother died at home, the morgue still required that his body be identified by a family member. My mother said she just could not go, so that left my sister and I to take care of it. We didn't know what to expect and all I could picture were the scenes from the television show, Quincy, when they visited the morgue and they would slide the draw out from the wall with the uncovered gross body in it. Thankfully, it wasn't that way at all.

When we arrived at the morgue, we had to walk down this very long hallway and I felt like Dorothy and Toto going down that long hallway in the Wizard of Oz when they were going to see the wizard. We were holding onto each other arm and arm, just so afraid of what we would see. Halfway down the hallway we could see my brother through a window, propped up on what looked like a hospital bed with his head wrapped in a white cloth. We confirmed to the person assisting us that it was in fact our brother Gregory Luther Williams, age 21. What a tragic loss for our family. He was such a funny person prior to the drug incident, always smiling and making jokes. It was very hard on my mother, who kept saying that she never wanted to bury one of her children because she expected her children to bury her.

The funeral arrangements were handled by Dallas Graham funeral home and we held the service the following Saturday at Royal Tabernacle Baptist Church, where my mother had since moved her membership from Mt. Ararat Baptist Church. My husband was able to join me in Jacksonville for the service, along with several of my church family members. I served on several auxiliaries at Pilgrim Baptist Church, including the choir, Young People's Auxiliary and weekly Bible Study student and later teacher. There were four cars of church family members who drove from Charleston to Jacksonville to support me during this tragic season of bereavement. They arrived the morning of the funeral and all I could do was cry when I saw the cars line up in front of the house on Moncrief Rd. These are the times when you need your spiritual family and they came through for me. They also turned around and drove back the same day, so they could be in church the next morning. I never forgot their labor of love and support and thanked them from the bottom of my heart.

My husband and I drove back the following Monday, but in separate cars, since I had been there a week before the funeral. I hated to leave my mother after such a tragedy, but she did have my two brothers, Ronald and Donald, as well as my sisters, Myrtia and Annette, to be with her since they all lived in Jacksonville.

Birth of My Second Son

After returning home, a few weeks later I found out that I was pregnant with my second child, due to be born in July of 1981. Death and life, the cycle continued. We had been trying to have another child, so I was very pleased with the news and prepared myself for the months ahead.

The pregnancy was uneventful from a health perspective and everything progressed normally, with the expectations of giving birth to a healthy baby. However, when I was eight months pregnant one major spiritual event occurred while I attended a revival in downtown Charleston. A visiting preacher, Pastor Ronald Brown, of Orangeburg, SC was in town conducting a revival and I did not want to miss it. So, my friend Mary and I hit the road in my little gray and black Toyota Corolla to attend the service. We were always traveling to some type of church service and put many miles on that Corolla because of it. I really enjoyed attending revivals and ministry conferences because my spiritual walk was maturing, and I had a hunger to know God in a deeper way. We had been attending weekly bible study at our church, Pilgrim Baptist, and were studying about the baptism of the Holy Spirit with the evidence of speaking in other tongues. Our leader was Rev. Frederick Hilton, and I remember him always being on fire for God and he already had the baptism and spoke in tongues. I wanted what he had. As we studied the scriptures, I knew there was more I wanted to experience, and

I wanted the baptism of the Holy Spirit we were studying about. We all did. Being in a Baptist Church, there was no teaching on the baptism of the Holy Spirit, so we had to study it on our own during our weekly bible study time at the church. Once the news got out that we were studying about "speaking in tongues", we were asked to stop having Bible study. Well we knew it was important for us to study the scriptures, so we just started having our study at each other's houses. It was a group of approximately seven to eight of us at the time and so we took turns hosting the bible study each week. We thought being booted out of the church for studying the Bible was just insane, but it did not stop us from seeking a deeper relationship with the Lord through studying His word. So, in June of 1981, in a very hot church in downtown Charleston, I received the Baptism of the Holy Spirit with the evidence of speaking in other tongues. I sometimes remind my son about that experience and let him know even though he tried to go another way as a teenager, he was in the presence of the anointing of the Holy Spirit before he was born so he was destined to serve the Lord.

A month later, on Sunday, July 26 at 1:30 p.m. my youngest son, Christopher Dewayne Joyce, was born into the world, weighing in at 8lbs and 5 ounces. He always seemed ahead of his time with what the older people called "an old soul". He grew into a fine young man and always amazed us with his knowledge and understanding at an early age. He could easily read when he was three turning four. We often couldn't wait until dinner time to see what he was going to share with us regarding his day. On one such occasion, when he was about four years old, he asked me what section I was in when I gave birth to him. I was confused by the question and asked him what did he mean by, "What section was I in"? He said he overheard his teacher saying that she was in the "C" section when she gave birth to her child, which caused my husband and me to both laugh. I explained to him that she was talking about "how" she gave birth to the baby rather than where she gave birth. I told him she had a C-section where they had to cut open her abdomen and remove the baby that way. Then he had to know how he was born, so I explained he was born through my birth canal, and I left it at that for a four-year-old. That story makes me laugh to this day. I was very grateful for the relationship my boys had with each other, especially since they were four years apart. They always looked out for the other one, especially if one was with me at the store and received a treat; they made sure I purchased one for the other. I loved the pictures I took of them when they were young sitting on the floor watching television and Chris would be sucking his thumb while rubbing his brother's ear lobe. We never understood why that was so comforting to him, but it was and apparently, his brother didn't mind. I like to think we made a good life for them growing up, even if I had some obsessive-compulsive issues with keeping the house clean. They were not allowed to leave toys on the floor after playing. They had to put them back in their designated area in their room or in the toy chest. I always made sure they were dressed very well and did not want for things they needed for school, as I did while growing up. As they grew older, it was evident that Derrick was more academic, and Chris was more creative, yet compassionate. They both started out in Christian School, but I later moved them to public school when Derrick was going to the 5th grade and Chris was in the first. The school they attended also accommodated handicapped children, and Chris was so moved by a little girl named Jessica who was in a wheelchair. He talked about her all the time and was so concerned about the fact that she couldn't walk and how he wanted to help her. I was glad to see he had a compassionate heart for others. Along with that compassionate heart was a tendency to be a free spirit in class, which didn't always sit well with the teacher, so I had to come up with a behavioral strategy to ensure he was doing what he needed to do in class. I met with the teacher after she sent notes home about Chris' behavior and I shared with her my plan. I made five large gold stars out of cardboard (about the size of the palm of one's hand) and gave them to the teacher. I instructed her to give him a star at the end of the day to bring home if his behavior was acceptable that day. If he didn't bring home a star he could not watch television with his brother, which he loved to do. She loved the idea and thanked me for taking the time to come up with something that taught him to realize consequences to his actions. We implemented the plan and it worked beautifully. Some days he received a star and then there were days he didn't, which caused him to be motivated the next day to keep his "free spirit" in check.

Derrick was very mindful of being obedient and a good student, which probably stemmed from me driving it into him that he had to get good grades, because he was going to Morehouse College in Atlanta GA (same school Dr. Martin Luther King, Jr. graduated) when he went to college. He always did very well in school, however, there was one report period in the 4th grade when he received a "D" in something, but I don't recall the subject. This was while he was still in the Christian school and their report cards were computer printouts with the class subjects listed beside the corresponding grades, along with the demographic information. Well, it took a brilliant mind to come up with this in the 4th grade, but he retyped his entire report card on our home computer and printed out a version with the "D" being changed to a "B", so I wouldn't find out he received a poor grade. Once it was brought to my attention what he did, I was upset more with myself than him because obviously I drove this child to go to the extreme to try to please me, which was not my intent. I was striving for perfection in him, which was unrealistic and I'm sure caused him more stress than necessary. It was important for him to understand the impact of what he did but I also had to acknowledge what led him to think he needed to do it. I'm more than grateful that neither of my sons were ever expelled from school, although Chris came close later during high school when he tried to live the thug life for a minute. Both played sports in school, basketball and football and were very good at both. When Chris was in the 9th grade, however, his grades were not up to the level they needed to be, and he was cut from the football team, which had a major impact on him. It was that change in his life, along with the fact that his father and I had separated again for the last time and had filed for divorce, which started him on a path which could have led to absolute destruction, "but God." He had a different destiny in store.

Death of My Mother

On March 10, 1986, my mother transitioned home to be with the Lord. She had just celebrated her 61st birthday on March 6. When you mother passes, you feel like you have no one left in the world who would be responsible for you, even though you're an adult. At least, I felt that way when my mother passed. I had sisters and brothers, a husband and children, but my mother, the person who gave me life, was no longer alive. I believe most of us feel that we can always count on our mother to be there for us and if anything, ever happened in your life you could go home to your mother. Well now, she was no longer on the earth and I had to take responsibility for myself, even though I had been doing so for years. I was thirty-one years old when my mother passed and for some reason for a moment, I felt like a little girl, and I didn't have a mother anymore.

My mother had been sick for many years with high blood pressure, disease of the coronary artery, rheumatoid arthritis, diabetes and renal failure. She had been on dialysis the last three years of her life and was living in an assisted living facility when she passed.

We were living in Charleston and after receiving the call, I packed up my sons and I drove during the night to be there the next morning to help my older sister with arrangements. I did not want her to deal with it alone, even for one day.

When death occurs in my family, I tend to shift into "take care of business" mode and don't usually spend a lot of time crying when there are things needing my attention. If you've ever planned a funeral you know there are several little and a few big things which must be done. First, you must choose a funeral home to pick up the body from the location where the person expired. Since my mother was friends with the Graham family, we chose Graham Mortuary to manage the funeral arrangements and they picked up my mother's body from the assisted living facility on the Southside of town on Old St. Augustine Rd. I now live not far from this facility in the Bartram Park area. Once they had the body, we then had to schedule time to meet with them to go over all the details of the funeral date, location, time, select a coffin and decide what my mother would be buried in. However, the first thing the funeral home want to know is how much insurance is available to cover the cost of their services. Thankfully, my mother believed in insurance and made sure her insurance was paid before she did anything else, which was a relief for us, her children. It's awful how some people don't believe in having insurance and when something happens to them their family is left trying to pull the funds together to take care of last expenses. Thankfully, we were not in that predicament.

Since my mother was a singer for many years we, agreed to bury her in a white coffin, white choir robe with a red stole, white gloves, and white pearl earrings. We also had to purchase new underwear, slip, and pantyhose; even though no one sees any of those things, its required by the funeral home. We were grateful to have my mother's best friend, whom we called Aunt Harry Mae to assist us with the details of the planning and service. She helped us to write the obituary and took care of planning the service with Pastor Robinson of Royal Tabernacle Baptist Church, where my mother was a member prior to being admitted to the assisted living facility. The service was planned for the Saturday after her passing. Typically, we have had funerals for our family members on Saturdays to allow people who work or need to come from out of town to attend. I was so surprised to have my boss, Diane, and several of my co-workers from Mass Mutual in Charleston SC, to drive to Jacksonville to support me during the service. It just warms your heart when people think enough of you to drive a distance to support you even though they didn't know my mother. I expressed my gratitude to all of them that day and upon my return to work a week later. The service was beautiful, and everyone talked about the awesome singing from my mother's friends during the service. The worse part of a funeral service for me is when they lower the coffin into the grave and begin to cover it up with dirt. This is when it hit me the hardest that I won't see my mother ever again on this side of heaven. I plan to see her when I get there.

My youngest sister was nineteen when our mother passed away, and she already had one son to whom she gave birth to at the age of 16. She and my mother were very close, in addition to my older sister, who relied on my mother a lot with one of her daughters who has cerebral palsy. My mother's guidance for them was going to be greatly missed, since there is nothing like the wisdom of your elders to help you along in the journey of life. I was not as close to my mother over the years since I moved to Charleston in 1977 and we only visited when there was a death in the family or when we were passing through to take the kids to Disney Land in Orlando. Other than the visit to Charleston when my second son was born, my mother wasn't able to spend a lot of time with my family over the years, so I did feel somewhat saddened by the fact that now she was gone and there would not be any future opportunities for her to get to know my children or broaden our relationship beyond the past experiences of some resentment for not protecting me from my brother. Nevertheless, my siblings and I vowed that we would make certain that we would try to get closer to each other and spend the next Christmas together, which we did, except for my youngest sister.

After my mother passed away, my youngest sister decided to move back to Philadelphia, where her father lived and hopefully establish a relationship with him, as well as allow him to get to know his grandson. We learned later that the bus trip to Philadelphia, ended up with her stopping in Washington DC and her being sweet talked into staying with a man there. He apparently was one of those people who preyed on young ladies traveling on Greyhound buses and presenting themselves as if they really didn't have anywhere to go. We were made aware later that in fact this guy was a pimp and he forced my sister into prostitution on the street. We didn't hear from her for a few years and by then she had given birth to other children, namely two girls. My oldest brother, Linwood who still lived in Philadelphia, along with his partner Charles, decided they would make a stop in Washington DC to try to see her on their drive back to Pennsylvania after a trip to Jacksonville. When they went to the apartment where she indicated she lived they said they saw blood on the door and there was no answer after several attempts of knocking. A neighbor opened their door and told them she wasn't there, and they didn't know where she was. They stated she would leave her small children home alone and be gone for hours and sometimes days. Well, my brother was panicked, not knowing what may have happened to them. Their next step was to go to the police station, which was a good thing since they were able to find out she was in protective custody. My brother explained who he was, and they allowed him to obtain the location to where she was being housed and allowed them to take her and the kids with them to Philadelphia.

When my brother shared all this information with my older sister, Myrtia, and me, we were just devastated. We never expected anything like this to happen to our baby sister. She and I agreed we would cover the cost of flying them all back to Jacksonville and they would stay with her until my youngest sister could find a place and get on her feet. We did just that and they returned to Jacksonville to live with my older sister for a while. I couldn't believe it but only three weeks had passed, and my sister was back on the bus again to Washington DC. We were horrified that she would make this decision after what she experienced and what her children had already endured. We could not believe it. We understood at the time that you cannot force someone to do the right thing and you can't want for them what they don't want for themselves. Therefore, we had to let it go and pray for her and her children from afar.

We often sit in judgement of others when their life does not align with what we expect but I reminded myself that I had no way of knowing what she truly was dealing with internally. I know how I felt when our mother passed away and I was 31 years old, but she was only 19. Could it have been that she thought she found a close-knit group of friends in Washington which filled the void of losing our mother or missing out on the love of a father while growing up? I don't know, but I also remind myself of the sins of my past and how God gave me several chances through His precious grace and I must train myself to do the same with others. Unless I've walked in their shoes I can't possibly speak their truth, either emotionally or mentally which may cause them to do what they do. I must love them through their mess as God loves me through mine.

By the time she had her fourth child-another son-things were difficult; she reached out for assistance from my sister, Myrtia, and me. Again, we were there to assist. We decided we would drive to Washington and take the oldest two children, a boy and a girl, leaving the two smaller children with her. My sister would take the boy and since I didn't have a girl, I would take the little girl. My sister's husband was open to the idea, but I had to convince my husband to allow me to bring another child home since it would be a major adjustment for our family. With a four-bedroom home, we had the room since my two sons shared a bedroom, my husband and I had our bedroom, we had a guest room and the fourth bedroom was practically storage. So, my sister drove from Jacksonville to Charleston with her four children and picked up me and my two boys and off we went to Washington DC. Thankfully, my sister had a brand-new van her husband bought her with some of his dog track winnings. It was very large and comfortable and made the trip a pleasant one. Our children were able to spend time together during the trip and after picking up our niece and nephew, we drove to Philadelphia to show our children where we grew up, went to school and visited some of our old friends from Paschal projects. There was one family we knew who still lived there, which was our friends' mother who had the twelve children, whose names began with "SH". She was very glad to see us and made lunch for all of us and called her daughter, Sharlene to come over and see us while we were in town. It was great to reconnect with someone I knew when I was a young girl. She turned out to be a fine young lady and was making a great life for herself and her family. The Paschal projects didn't look the same since the buildings were old and the yards were un-kept. When we took the kids to see our school, John Bartram High School, we were amazed at how small it looked compared to how it looked when we were students there. I guess since we were larger it seemed smaller. Although the reason for our adventure was not the most ideal of circumstances, the trip turned out to be one of the best times I experienced with my sister and our combined families, minus husbands. With additions to each of our families we headed back to South Carolina first to drop off my crew and then my sister drove on to Jacksonville after a rest period.

It was exciting to have a little girl to take care of, and I wanted to make sure we made a good life for her. I decorated her room for a little girl, and we all tried to settle into this new life. My boys loved having a little sister and my niece was thrilled to have a family, with a father figure in the home, her own room and nice clothes to wear. Once I shared with my co-workers that I brought my four-year-old niece to live with me, they gave me a youth shower. I couldn't call it a baby shower since she was not a baby. I was so very grateful for the clothes, toys and love they showered on us during that time. I enrolled my niece into the four-year-old class at the school run by my church at the time, Glad Tidings Assembly of God. She loved school, but it was evident early that she had some learning difficulties and understandably so since there had not been any stability in her life up to that point. I worked with her as much as I possibly could, and it was a big difference from my boys who both were excellent readers and had good math skills. My niece, Tanita, lived with our family for two years, and when it was time for me to enroll her into public school for the first grade, her mother refused to give me guardianship even though I had been taking care of her for the past two years. Apparently, she still claimed her on her benefits in Washington, and if she gave me guardianship, it would cut her benefits. I, therefore, had no choice but to take this sweet little girl back to her mother in Washington DC. It broke my heart, as well as my sons and even my husband was used to having her around by then. I cried most of the drive to Washington and could not believe her mother; my sister would rob this child of a comfortable life because of a few dollars. Nevertheless, I did not want to fight her for her own child. Now years later, it's evident her life would have turned out differently if she had been raised in our home compared to how she was raised. This often happens in families. Parents don't always do what's best for the children, but usually what's best for them. Again, you can't want for someone what they don't want for themselves. Tearfully I turned her over to her mother and drove back to Charleston to carry on life with my husband and two sons.

Years later, while attending nursing school, my marriage had unfortunately taken a turn for the worse. My husband began to be very jealous and accused me of seeing other people. While in nursing school, I had my classes, clinical assignments, worked 20 hours per week, had to be a wife and take care of two children. On the days prior to clinical training in the hospital, I would spend hours at the hospital the evening before to obtain patient assignments and gather needed information to develop care plans for each. This usually resulted in me staying up most of the night to prepare, studying medications, diagnoses, and treatment protocols for all my assigned patients so I would be able to respond appropriately when my instructor drilled me. I was totally exhausted most of the time and for him to accuse me of being out with someone when I walked in the door after those long days of class, work, and clinical assignments, it was more than I could handle. Even when I went to church, he accused me of being with the pastor. If I had a close girl friend at work, he accused me of being a lesbian. It had gotten so bad that he placed a voice-activated recorder under our bed. I found out about that from my youngest son, which then caused them to have a strained relationship during that time. I was already unhappy, and this just was getting to be too much. I still hung in there until about a year after I graduated but then reached a point when I said to myself, "I am going to either commit suicide or I need to leave him again for good." I had gone down the path of wanting to commit suicide some years prior, which caused me to end up admitted to Medical University of SC Psychiatric unit for help dealing with my depression and suicidal ideations. I'll never forget that ordeal and those dark days.

Plan to Commit Suicide

The first time I considered suicide I was working at the life insurance company. I was so depressed and sad about my life, although I was now the office manager, had a good salary, home, family etc. but still had a big hole in my soul. It was a dark season and I could not see hope for the future. It felt like it was always going to be that way and there was no hope for a better life for me. When you're in that black hole of depression you just can't seem to bring yourself to a hopeful state of mind. I therefore made a plan that on one Friday evening after I got home I would take the gun out of my husband's trunk, which he stored in the guest room and I was going to end my life. Up to this point, I had never touched a gun and didn't know how to use one, but I figured it couldn't be that difficult. Well Friday came, and I was a bit anxious that morning as I sat at my desk in my office at work, just going through the motions of working, all the while thinking none of it would matter because I would not be back on Monday. I would be dead. Around 1:00 p.m. that day, my receptionist called into my office and stated that there was someone at the front desk to see me. I couldn't image who it could be since I had no appointments. I just told her to send them back since my office was just around the corner from the front desk. Standing in the doorway of my office was a friend of mine named Donna, a white young lady I used to work with and had not seen for at least six months. She asked if she could come in and speak to me about something and I said sure. In my depressed state, I did not have the energy to be overly excited to see her even though it was good to see her. She closed the door to my office, remained standing, and said she had been praying and the Lord impressed upon her strongly to come to my office and to tell me not to do it and that He loves me. She stated she didn't know what I was going to do but His prompting was so strong she could not ignore it. I immediately burst into tears because I had not spoken to anyone about what I was planning to do so it surely had to be God who spoke to her to come. I shared with her what I had planned to do that evening and we both cried and embraced knowing that we have a heavenly Father who loves us so much He would interrupt her prayer and speak to her heart about his other daughter who was in so much pain and planned to take her life. It was at that very moment that I understood how much God truly loved me for real. No more group Christianity. He loves me as an individual and He spoke my name to my friend Donna, who drove from North Charleston to downtown to tell me. I often think what would have happened if she had just blown it off, as we sometimes do when a task is assigned to us that seems uncomfortable. I thank God she didn't and was obedient to the prompting and followed through. When I got home that night, instead of taking my own life, I sat on the side of my bed and read Romans 5:8 aloud to myself repeatedly until it took root in my heart. I personalized it by placing my name where it referenced the world and whosoever, so it read;

"But God demonstrated His love towards Lynette, in that while Lynette was still a sinner, Christ died for Lynette." To this day, my life is bearing a harvest because of the truth of that word and the miracle that took place in my office that Friday I planned to end it all.

Although I embraced the miracle that occurred, I knew I still needed help because I could not sort out my feelings and didn't understand how to move beyond where I was. I felt like I was having a nervous breakdown, because my body didn't have the energy to move. I recall going to the bathroom the following week while at work and could not bring myself to move my limbs to readjust my clothing to leave the bathroom. It was like my body said you have stressed me to the point of shutdown. It must have taken me 30 minutes to get it together so once I returned to my office, I called my doctor. I explained what occurred and she referred me to Medical University of SC Psychiatric Facility for evaluation and treatment. My husband and my children could not understand where I was emotionally, and I could not fully explain it either but knew I needed help. I was admitted to the facility and stayed for approximately two weeks. The group therapy as well as the one-on-one therapy sessions were very helpful, and I began to climb out of that black hole, little by little. I was able to express and discuss a lot of feelings from my past experiences and the impact they had on me, which I didn't realize but God has a way of chipping away at that old fallow ground, so we can become pliable to allow Him to finish molding us as we spin on that potter's wheel. It took a while, but with a lot of prayer, the use of anti-depressants and ongoing outpatient therapy I reached the other side where there was light and droplets of hope for a better future. Oftentimes when people ask me why I smile so much, I laugh on the inside because I know there was a time when I couldn't so I'm grateful to be able to now.

Decision to Leave

I had vowed not to allow myself to get so depressed about external circumstances it caused me to want to end my life. Yet here I was again approximately a year after graduating nursing school feeling so depressed about my life that the choice to end it surfaced again. However, this time I gathered all the strength within me and made the brave decision to leave my husband again, but this time it was for good.

I purchased a mobile home, rented a U-Haul truck and my husband watched me move my things along with my youngest sons for the last time. Derrick was away at Morehouse College by this time and I wanted to make sure he could continue his education despite what was going on at home. This meant I took on another job working 12 days on and 2 days off. During the week, I worked as a clinical review nurse for a health insurance company and on the weekends, I pulled two evening shifts working for a home health agency.

Altogether, I probably left my husband about four times during our 22-year marriage. One of the biggest challenges I faced with leaving him and filing for divorce was with the church. The church always preached to stay together no matter what and do not get a divorce. I never intended to be divorced or wanted my children to have a broken family but there comes a time when one must rule in favor of oneself. I knew what it was to have a friend commit suicide. Her husband abused her horribly, and she felt like she couldn't leave because of what the church preached and taught. This young lady jumped off an overpass and was hit by a tractor-trailer truck, leaving three children behind. I could not comprehend it at the time. Why didn't the church love her better? It is so critically important not to take scripture out of context and judge others when you haven't walked a day in their shoes. I know God hates divorce, but He also wants us to be at peace and if I can't have peace then there is no need to be with a person. Everyone must answer for the choices they make in life and even when we make bad choices, I'm so thankful that God is a God of second chances. Getting a divorce is not the worst thing you can do, I think it's worse to stay in a situation where you're already divorced mentally, physically and most of all emotionally. Peace is a wonderful thing.

I would be remiss in writing my story to leave you believing that my first husband was a horrible man, because it just was not the case. He was a good man, who worked hard and tried to provide a good home for his family. However, he could not give me what I felt I needed, even as unrealistic as it may have been at the time. The hole that was so big in my soul could not be filled by him or any other man. Only God can fill the hole in any man or woman's soul. We often try to fill it with relationships, alcohol, drugs, adventures, work, sex etc. etc. but true deliverance comes when we finally acknowledge and allow God, the creator of the universe, to come and fill up that hole with his pure love, as only He can do. It is unfair for us to expect others to do so, when they don't have the capacity or the assignment to do it. At the age of 19 when I married, I had no idea of what real love looked or felt like. I'm sure he was very frustrated at times trying to figure out how to love me because he only knew of one way and that was to provide a home, as a good husband would. When that wasn't enough or what I felt I needed, he reacted in the only way he knew how, to resort to attacks, sometimes verbal, sometimes physical, and often emotional. Due to the fact I was so broken, he would have needed to be a Christian psychologist to understand the depth of my brokenness and how to appropriately respond to me to prevent further brokenness. After leaving and spending time with the Lord in a more peaceful environment, I was able to gain insight into this and I wrote my husband a six-page letter expressing what I had come to understand and to ask his forgiveness for my part in our broken marriage. He never responded and from that point on we remained somewhat cordial when our paths crossed. I always wished him well and hoped that he would find someone to love again. At the time of this writing, he has not remarried and knowing his makeup, he may not trust his heart to another woman since I was his second wife. I will always respect him as the father of my two sons and only want the best for his future.

Death of My Sister

My sister was my first best friend. Growing up no one thought we were sisters, especially in school, because we didn't act like typical sisters but more like best friends. We ended up in the same grade because I skipped kindergarten and went straight into first grade and since she was only one year older than me she too was in the first grade. When we saw each other in the hallways we greeted each other like we hadn't seen each other in days, hugging and laughing like to two little school girls. At home, my sister tried to be my protector when it came to my brother hurting me. She was often unsuccessful but at least she tried, and I loved her for trying. We talked about everything and as we got older, we loved to read those love story magazines during the summer, as well as long novels, like Gone with the Wind, which would help get us through the summer months since there were no vacations for us. Of course, there was the occasional funeral we attended in Jacksonville when a close relative passed away but no real vacations. My sister was tough when it came to standing up to our mother whenever we got in trouble for one thing or another. No matter how old we were, my mother didn't mind taking the belt to us and my sister was able to stand there without shedding a tear while getting a beating. I on the other hand would start crying while my mother was moving in my direction to beat me. I often ran into the closet and tried to hold the door so she couldn't get in but that just made her angrier and the beating would be worse. I used to ask my sister how she could stand there and get a beating without crying and she would tell me she didn't want to give my mother the satisfaction of knowing she was hurting her. There were years my sister was more of a home body and I was more active outdoors, jumping double Dutch or going to the skating rink, but in the evenings, we always stayed up talking about our day and everything else which crossed our minds.

When we were around 15 and 16 respectively, we traveled to Willow Grove Park with our family and many of our neighbors, since it was a neighborhood outing. We had community trips in those days, where all the neighbors planned a trip for the families, rented a large bus, made the arrangements and off we'd go. This trip, my sister and I had planned to meet up with these two guys who lived in the neighborhood and planned to go on the trip but didn't want to ride on the bus with the rest of us. They drove to the park and we met them there. The plan was to leave the park and ride around but return before the bus left to return to Philly. Well we never counted on the car breaking down and missing the bus to get back home. We were in panic mode, knowing that our mother was going to kill us when we finally made it home. The guys were able to fix the car and we arrived back home late that evening. When they let us out in front of our house, my brothers were on the front steps and quickly said "Ooh, yawl are going to get it." which we already knew. When we walked in the house my mother already had the belt ready and she tore into us like there was no tomorrow. As a parent now, I can imagine how scarred she probably was when we didn't show up to the bus when everyone was leaving because she didn't know if something had happened to us and she didn't want to leave us there or if we were off gallivanting with these guys as we were. Man, we learned our lesson from that experience and we had the whelps to show for it. There was no child abuse in those days since the understanding was if you sparred the rod you spoiled the child and we were in no way spoiled.

After my mother moved back to Jacksonville in 1973, a few months later my aunt Leola, introduced my sister, Myrtia, to a guy (Lonnie), whom would later become her husband. My aunt worked with him at the Evergreen Cemetery and thought they would make a nice couple. They hit it off and a few months later got married. I was happy for her and was glad that she didn't have to work, but stay home and take care of her family. She already had her daughter, Tamika, which was born in Philadelphia, and she quickly gave birth to her second child, another girl, named Tiffany. The second daughter unfortunately was born with cerebral palsy and required special care, which included surgeries soon after birth. My mother helped my sister with her care and her husband was very helpful as well. She later gave birth to two more children, another girl, Tasha, and a boy, named Alonzo. They were only 10 months apart, which caused some people to see them as twins. We both began to live our separate lives and manage our families, but always stayed in touch by phone, even when my family moved to Charleston.

I remember visiting my sister one year, while we were on our way to our yearly vacation spot in Orlando, and she asked me what I thought about taking out cancer insurance. At the time I said to her "I don't think I need cancer insurance because I don't plan on getting cancer". We laughed, and I will always remember her saying, "well I think I'm going to take out some insurance just in case". At the time she had no idea that a few years later, she would develop breast cancer and indeed need that insurance.

When my sister called me to tell me she was diagnosed with breast cancer, I initially thought she would beat it and everything would be all right. She would call me and read to me the results of her tests and the treatments she was receiving, and I would be back and forth with the doctors asking questions to get a good understanding of where she was in the progression of the disease. As a nurse, I understood the staging and realized that it didn't look good, however, the plan was for her to have a double mastectomy, start chemotherapy and radiation and go from there. I made sure I was there for the surgery and stayed a few days with her after discharge but had to return to Charleston since Chris was in school, and I had to work. As the months went on, her prognosis got worse and the cancer had metastasized to her bones, which was very painful for her.

I'll never forget when I received the call during what ended up being her last hospitalization. I was at work and received a call from her doctor stating that she was in the hospital and things didn't look good. I was trying to decide when I would leave for Jacksonville, either that day or the next day. One of my co-workers said to me, "Lynette, if I were you I would leave today." When she said it, I just had a feeling she was right, so I left work immediately ran home packed a few things and got on the road for Jacksonville. I arrived in her hospital room and she was still conscious, which allowed us to talk and just have a beautiful time reminiscing about old times and there was such a sense of peace and sweetness that filled the room. I stayed the night with her at the hospital as I often did when she was admitted, and this time was no different. The next morning, she slipped into unconsciousness and the doctor told us he would release her home with hospice because it would not be long. I was so grateful to my co-worker who talked me into leaving the day before, so I had those precious moments with her because that was the last time we were able to have a conversation.

I requested time off from work, because I was not going to leave her side during this critical time and her husband needed to keep his job, as the only breadwinner for their family. At the time, my oldest niece was in college and her two youngest children were seniors in high school. Her son was an all-American football player with a full scholarship to Marshall University in West Virginia. It was devastating for them to see their mom in her condition. We ordered a hospital bed for her home to keep her comfortable and hospice was initiated. I planned to stay the remainder of that week, but return home on Friday to get more clothes, take care of a few things and return to Jacksonville on Sunday, which I did.

As I turned down Dillon Street to my sister's house, I saw several cars out in front of her house and I said to myself, "why are all those people there, they act like she's already dead." I pulled into the driveway and my niece ran out of the house crying saying, Auntie, Momma passed away about 30 minutes ago". My heart sank to the ground. There was a flood of emotions that came over me at that moment. My sister was gone, and I wasn't there. I felt horrible. How could I not be there when she passed after being there all week? I only went home to get more clothes and take care of some things. If only I had left earlier from Charleston, I would have been there when she transitioned. I ran into the house and found that indeed she had passed. I held her hand, told her I loved her, and I'll see her on the other side. I quickly shifted gears and began to see to her children that needed comforting, as well as her husband. I confirmed that the hospice nurse had been called and notification made to the funeral home. We waited for the body to be removed and we all stood there, knowing our lives had changed forever. My dear sweet sister, my first best friend in the world transitioned into eternity on Sunday evening, November 10, 1996 at the young age of 42 years old.

The next morning, I began to make the necessary calls to plan for the service before meeting with the funeral director of Huff Funeral Home. The first call I made was to the church where she had been a member but unable to attend since being diagnosed with breast cancer. I wasn't ready for the response I received from the pastor of the church when I informed him of her passing and if we could plan the service at his church. He informed me that since she had not been in attendance for almost a year she was no longer considered a member. I said, "Sir, my sister was diagnosed with breast cancer in January and have been in and out of the hospital for months. If you kept in touch with your members you would have known that." I then said, "Forget it, I'll work something else out," and hung up the phone. It's sad when ministers forget to whom they are called, and people are not called to them. I reached out to my sister's friend who lived down the street and whose minister visited her several times while she was in the hospital. When I informed her, what occurred with my sister's church, she immediately said "Oh let me place a call to my pastor, I'm sure he will assist." She promised to get right back with me, which she did in about ten minutes. She had scheduled time for my sister's husband and me to meet with the pastor that day, a few hours later to be exact.

When we met with him, he expressed his condolences and assured us that it would not be an issue for us to have my sister's funeral at his church. He offered for the choir to sing, the ushers to serve, preparation of the program, use of their fellowship hall for the repast and he would be honored to do the eulogy. He spoke about how he enjoyed visiting my sister when she was in the hospital and knew of her love for the Lord. We were so grateful for this true expression of the love of Christ and thanked him for his generosity, especially since my sister had never even set foot one time into his church. He was an example of a Godly minister, here to serve the people of God without reservation. He didn't ask for any money but only the opportunity to serve the family in our time of bereavement. We were blown away when the service took place the following Saturday because the entire choir was in the choir stand, the ushers were on their post and these people prepared the food for the family to be served at the repast. I was so pleased that my sister's service was filled with such Christian love by these dear sweet people of Greater Jacksonville Church of God, who had never even met her but willing to serve. Only the pastor of the church, Rev. Dr. Rene Evans, Jr. had met her and knew her well enough to give a beautiful eulogy. I too spoke on behalf of my sweet sister, as well as her daughter with cerebral palsy also said a few words. It was a beautiful service and I know she was well pleased. Things always work out for the best in the end. God is faithful and will not leave His children lacking.

Prior to my sister's passing, her husband did not go to church or serve the Lord. However, due to the out pouring of love from this church and pastor, my brother-in-law started attending their church and gave his life to the Lord. I'd like to think this was one positive outcome of my sister's passing. I also vowed to sow financially into their ministry as often as I was able to do so, and I did for months after.

A couple of years after my sister's passing, my brother-in-law met a young lady at the church, and they got married and are still married to this day.

A Story of Real Forgiveness

In July of 2002, I purchased my first home on my own. I was so proud of myself since this was actual property (not like the mobile home I had previously purchased and allowed my youngest son and his friend to rent). It was a beautiful, two-story starter home with three bedrooms, formal living room, dining room, breakfast nook, family room, Florida room and large back yard. The former owner was an older single female who was no longer able to tolerate the stairs in the house, but left it move-in ready. I took great pride in caring for the yard and making sure everything inside the house was well kept. I love a neat home and would spend hours cleaning on Saturdays before tackling the yard.

Well, I had only been moved into my home approximately one month before receiving a call from the hospital in Altoona PA, where my oldest brother, Linwood lived. He had been admitted to ICU for an overdose of insulin, and they were trying to reach the next of kin. This is the same brother who physically abused me throughout my young life, starting with the time he hit me in the head with a brick when I was a young toddler. I still have the scars on my hands and thighs from when he held me against our heater until my flesh burned, creating pus filled blisters. He would punch me in my head with his fists, verbally abuse me, stabbed me in the face once, and I often endured raged filled attacks. This was my life for years, but now I received a call that he's in ICU. Being a Christian and thinking

I had forgiven him years before for all these things, I pulled myself together and flew up to Altoona to be by his side and do what I could to manage his affairs, awaiting the outcome of this illness.

He had several physical issues, which I wasn't totally aware of, in addition to being an insulin dependent diabetic. He had high blood pressure, cardiac disease, renal failure, blood clots and low blood counts, but pulled through and was discharged to a nursing home for recovery and I returned home.

A few weeks later, I received another call from the doctors indicating that due to all his health issues they suggest he no longer live alone, and he needed to be discharged to a family member's care. Well since my older sister had passed away, my two brothers being merchant seamen were always out to sea, and my younger sister was not able to take him in, it was up to me to be the caregiver.

How could this be? I was just enjoying my new home and now I was going to take my brother in and care for him? The one who hurt me for so many years. Well, yes that's exactly what was about to take place and I didn't know how I was going to handle it. I prayed for God to give me the grace to deal with this person I hated and feared for years.

Plans were made, and the facility flew him from Altoona PA to Charleston SC and I met him at the airport. When I saw him, I was amazed because he was a shell of a man in a wheelchair. I gathered all his luggage and brought him to my home and to his bedroom. Once he was settled, I had to have a heart to heart with him because I had not been around him for years, except for the visit to the hospital a few weeks before. I told him that he was now in my house and it was only because of the Jesus in me that he was even in my home, however, I would do what I had to do to take care of him but there had to be some rules. He would not ever raise his voice to me, strike me in any way, or lay around in pajamas all day. He would need to dress every day, keep himself clean, and he would be expected to go to church with me on Sundays, unless he was sick. He stated he understood and agreed. I still felt so uneasy in his presence, which let me know that I really had not truly forgiven him because fear was still in my belly. I hated feeling like this in my own home. The worse thing about this was I had no way of knowing how long I would need to endure this situation. I made his breakfast, set up meals on wheels for his lunch and cooked dinner every night. I washed his clothes, took him to the many doctor appointments and kept track of the 14 medications and injections he took each day. I would literally cry every night because I could not believe God would require me to do this after how he treated me all my life.

One night when I was crying in my bathroom, I heard God speak to me clearly saying, "How you handle this will determine your level in ministry." At this point, I said to myself, "Well I guess I had better suck it up and get through this with God's help because I could not do it on my own. He also revealed to me that He had to set this circumstance up so that I could learn to truly forgive whom I thought was unforgivable. He said, "You have been called to help write the last chapter of his life." With this as my motivation and inspiration, I settled in to do what I had to do to care for my brother.

One Saturday in January 2003, I had to go into my work office and later planned to go to a birthday celebration for my then daughter-in-law. So, I got up early and prepared my brother's breakfast and placed it on the table in the breakfast nook. I called upstairs and told him it was ready, so he could come down and eat. I told him I wouldn't be back until late in the evening since I had plans after I leave the office. I arrived back home around 7:30 p.m. And when

I opened the door, I could see the breakfast I had made early that morning still in the place I left it. A sense of horror came over me because I thought, oh my goodness, I hope he's not upstairs dead. So, I called out to him, with no answer. I slowly climbed the stairs not sure what I would find once I reached the top. I could hear a faint whimpering coming from his room and upon opening the door, there he was on the floor curled up in an almost fetal position but still alive. I quickly shifted into rescue mode and lifted him off the floor back onto the bed (he was very thin) only to realize he had soiled himself. I began asking him what happened, and he was trying to tell me his head was hurting, and he fell onto the floor when he got up that morning. I felt bad since I was gone all day, and he had been on the floor all day. I picked him up in my arms and carried him to the bathtub, so I could clean him up, but knew I needed to take him to the hospital for evaluation. Once I had him in the water and bathed him, I placed the call to 911 since there was no way I could carry him downstairs to drive him in my car. It took approximately 15 minutes for the ambulance to arrive, which allowed me time to put a fresh pair of pajamas on him and get him ready for the paramedics to carry him down the stairs for transport. I followed in my car and met them in the emergency room. After examination and a few scans, it was determined he had a brain hemorrhage, and he would be admitted for further evaluation.

This, in fact, was the last time my brother was in my home. He ended up staying in the hospital for several weeks and then he had to be transferred to a nursing home because he could not care for himself at all. At the same time, my job was being eliminated, and I was looking for another job. It could not have been a more stressful time, but I trusted God to see me through it all.

At this time, I had been working as a Director of Health Services with CIGNA healthcare and our jobs were being eliminated. I had worked my way up the ladder from a claims review nurse, to a pre-service review nurse, to a Concurrent review nurse, to a Case Manager, to a local trainer, then to regional trainer, to a corporate transformation specialist and then to Director of Health Services, over a seven-year period. Based upon the experience I acquired over the years with CIGNA, I was contacted by a recruiter from Blue Cross Blue Shield in Atlanta for a Director of Medical Operations position which they had open at the time. I went to Atlanta, interviewed for the position and was offered a very lucrative package to assume the role, which I accepted. Thankfully, the package included a sign on bonus, relocation package, which included selling my home without me attending the closing, moving and storing my furniture, as well as assistance purchasing a home in Atlanta. They even housed me for two months in an apartment with a concierge that costed the company $2K per month. I felt so privileged to be treated in this manner and believe my obedience in caring for my brother opened that door and the favor that followed.

I had no way of knowing when I took my brother in that it would only be for a period of five months that I had to take care of him in my home. During that time, God allowed me to see him in a different light, in that I was helping to write the last chapter of his life. I began to feel sorry for him because he had been a tormented human being, which caused him to be the way he was growing up. He had been raped at the age of 16 by a man who hired him to help cater a large event, which opened the door for him to live a homosexual life style. He had a very tumultuous relationship with his partner, Charles, even though they were together for over 20 plus years. When Charles had enough of my brother's behavior, he left him and never looked back, which I know deeply affected him. My heart began to soften towards him and even more so when I arrived home to find him on the floor suffering from a brain hemorrhage, knowing I left him alone all day. Upon visiting him in the hospital, I would talk to him about his spiritual state since he no longer was able to go to church and during one of those visits took him through the sinner's prayer to salvation. Once I did that, my heart grew more and more open to loving him rather than fearing and hating him. I was so grateful to God that by the time I had to place him in a nursing home and relocate to Atlanta, I could tell him I loved him and meant it. I had truly forgiven him for all the things he had done to me and it was a liberating experience. God reminded me that he brought about the circumstance so that I could be free and no longer walk in a false sense of forgiveness, as I had been. If he would not have been living in my home with me, I don't think I would have ever really forgiven him like I did. God always knows what He's doing, even when we don't understand initially.

I started my new job as Director of Medical Operations with Blue Cross Blue Shield of Georgia, purchased a brand new beautiful 3,100 square foot home in the Arbor Glen subdivision of Conyers and began my life in Atlanta. It was a major adjustment, but I was excited to be there and gave it my all. Approximately four weeks into the transition, I received a call from the hospital in Charleston telling me that my brother had been admitted from the nursing home and they wanted to make me aware. I advised them I would be there the weekend to check on him, but it was only a couple days later they called and told me he had passed away. To my shock and dismay, on Wednesday, April 13th my brother passed away at the age of 51 years old. He would have been 52 his next birthday on May 18th but didn't make it. I asked if they could leave his body in the room until I drove from Atlanta and they said they could. I notified my family and let them know I was on my way to Charleston as soon as I could get there, and they should meet me at the hospital.

When I arrived at the hospital, it was surreal to go into the room knowing he had passed away and entered eternity. It all flooded back to me how God warned me that I had been called to help write the last chapter of his life, not knowing it would end so quickly, but I'm sure God knew. I am so grateful he accepted Jesus into his heart and was saved before passing away. Our coming together was two-fold; for me it was to truly forgive so that God could take me to the next level in preparation for my assignment in Atlanta and for him to free himself of the guilt and shame he walked in and accept Jesus as Lord and Savior of his life.

I found myself planning yet another funeral, including covering the cost because my brother had no life insurance. I had a short service in Charleston and then had my brother's body shipped to Jacksonville FL for a graveside ceremony, which I officiated, and finally laid his body to rest in Edgewood Cemetery on Edgewood Ave.

When I think about all God accomplished in my life and my brother's life over a nine-month period, my faith is strengthened, and I understand how God loves us, even those whom we think aren't loveable. He loved my brother enough that he humbled him, so he would need to receive care from the very person he abused for so many years and allowed that same person to lead him to salvation, giving him eternal life. He humbled me to see that to walk in true ministry one must know how to forgive for real, just as He forgave us. I pray to this day that my heart stays open to walk in forgiveness and not in judgement. I thought it was a lesson too hard to learn because every night I cried out to God, asking "WHY" He would require me to care for someone who cared so little for me. At the end of the day, I want to mature to be Christ like and forgive, understanding that "they know not what they do". Therefore, what the enemy meant for evil God turned around for our good.

Atlanta and My Second Marriage

It was a Thursday evening in February 2003, when I drove into Atlanta Georgia in my white Plymouth Breeze, ready to start a new life in a new city. Inside, I was scared because of all the unknowns. Would I like my new job? Would I like living in Atlanta? Would I make lasting friendships? The one known certainty I was excited and glad to attend New Birth Missionary Baptist Church, where Bishop Eddie Long was the Pastor. This was one of the reasons I accepted the job because I could attend New Birth. I used to watch Bishop Long on television on Sunday mornings before going to church when I lived in Charleston. He had a unique ministry style and always seemed relevant to current events. Most ministers don't dare speak out on the issues of the day, for they want to play it safe and not ruffle anyone's feathers, at least not the governmental or social powers. But that was not Bishop Long. He was on it in a real way and I looked forward to being under his ministry.

Nevertheless, I had a big job ahead of me with taking on the role of Director of Medical Operations with Blue Cross Blue Shield of Georgia. It was the best financial offer I'd had up to this point in my career. With the sign-on bonus, I would hit six-figures, and with all the other benefits, it was an offer I could not refuse. The company sold my house in Charleston without me attending the closing but forwarded me the check for my equity, moved my furniture, and stored it until I purchased a home in Atlanta; they even provided a realtor to assist as well as paid a portion of the closing cost on the new home. They also covered the cost of a furnished apartment until I was able to purchase my home. Overall, it was a sweet deal and I was excited to get my new life started.

I had been in Atlanta approximately eight months, when during one Wednesday night service at New Birth, I met a gentleman by the name of Nelson. We were standing in line together in the bookstore and I noticed that he looked at me rather strangely when I looked his direction while awaiting my turn in line. He then approached me, asked my name, and introduced himself. We made small talk and he told me he had moved to Georgia from California, he was a Pastor and in the process of starting a new church in Augusta. After we made our purchases, he asked if he could sit with me during the service, which I was not too thrilled about because I didn't like anyone interfering with my worship service. I wanted to focus on the Lord and enjoy the praise and worship without talking or considering someone I just met. Nevertheless, I agreed. At the end of the service we exchanged information and I informed him that I would be taking a class at the church the following Saturday. As fate would have it, he also had something related to his church, which was coming under the leadership of Bishop Long, the same day and time. While in my class, I happened to turn around in the class and who do I see but this guy. My first thought was he's stalking me, but, at the same time, I was flattered. Again, we made small talk after the class and decided to have lunch together, which was the start of a dating relationship. He informed me that the Lord spoke to him the night we met in the bookstore at New Birth, saying I was the wife God had prepared for him, which is why he looked at me so strangely the night we met. It took me by surprise, but again I was flattered. I was a bit awestruck because he was a Pastor and people often said that I would marry a Pastor or Bishop. I began to think God allowed me to move to Atlanta, attend New Birth to bring us together and I would be a first lady. I kind of liked the idea and he seemed to be a nice guy. He always dressed in a suit so there was no issue with his attire and I like to see men in suits, however, I wasn't sure every day was necessary, but he called it his uniform as a Pastor.

One Friday evening, he came by my house and provided me with evidence to justify who he was, which included his military honorable discharge, his divorce papers from his first and only wife, his degree from his masters program and ordination ceremony to become a minister. I was somewhat impressed that he felt the need to do this, but he explained that since we recently met, and he believed I was to be his wife, then he needed to make certain I knew he was the real deal. He asked me what type of rings I liked, and I answered as if in a general discussion, saying I always liked marquise shaped diamonds. Within approximately three weeks, he had purchased me a 2-carat marquise shaped diamond ring and asked me to marry him. Wow. This was going very fast, but I thought, this must be God since he heard God say I was his wife, he's a Pastor, and I'm a woman of God; this will be my opportunity to be a first lady and help build a ministry. I had always worked with other ministries helping to build other houses but also felt like there was a call on my life for ministry as well. Could this be why I was in Atlanta? I had prayed for a Godly relationship because ministry was very important to me, however, sometimes we spiritualize things and don't take time to do a reality check.

We continued to date, and it was Christmastime when I decided to take him to Charleston to meet my family, friends and Pastors at the church where I would want to be married. The introductions went very well, and everyone was very happy for me. Plans were underway to be married the following June in Charleston. I started attending church with him on Sundays in Augusta GA but we both went to New Birth on Wednesday evenings for mid-week service. I was introduced to his congregation as his fiancé, and I was very engaging with his members. I was excited to think of working with these people to do ministry and grow the church. I loved outreach, so I could see us going out into the streets of Augusta ministering to the needs of the people and inviting them to service on Sundays. I felt like God had His hand on us.

I did notice how he would watch me as I interacted with the members of the church, but he never said anything negative about it. I am a people person and I enjoy engaging with people, especially those I feel led to minister to and give of myself in some way. Apparently, this must have bothered him for some reason, because he reached out to my Pastors from my church in Charleston and was inquiring about my service and interactions within their ministry. I suppose the conversation led him to believe that I was a strong woman and didn't mind saying what I needed to say when I needed to say it, which, from my perspective, is not a bad thing, but for some men, not so much. He later called me and told me that the wedding was off and that he felt like I would try to take over his church. Wow. I was blindsided with this one, but he explained about his conversation with my Pastor in Charleston and how he noticed how I interacted with the members, how they gravitated to me, and he could not allow this. Obviously, I was hurt and devastated, not to mention embarrassed due to the announcement of the engagement to family, friends and co-workers.

My thoughts immediately went to, "what is wrong with me"? I master most things in my life such as career, friendships, finances but for some reason I continue to fail at love relationships. Well, here I was now in Atlanta and still failed at love.

As I was accustomed, I buried the pain and pulled it together because I had a lot of work ahead of me with my job and commitments. I gave him his ring back, although I contemplated keeping it out of spite, but at the end of the day, I just couldn't do it. What I thought was God's hand, was not. My faith started to waiver because I misread the leading of the Holy Spirit, or did I? Perhaps, was it supposed to be, but man's will, pride and jealousy got in the way? I'll never know but learned from the experience to fully seek the face of God for my own life and not trust what God supposedly said to someone else about my life.

From a work perspective, there was a lot to be done, but I love a challenge and jumped right into the day-to-day efforts to clear up the chaos as quickly as possible. I quickly realized there were several hindrances to success, which included a great divide between the Atlanta office and the Columbus office and the number of staff available to perform the duties was not enough. This is typical for most corporations, they want you to work with less than enough staffing and yet expect excellent results. I worked with a great group of staff members and was often told they looked at me as Moses, who came to take them into the Promised Land. I was the first black Director of Medical Operations for this office. I made it a point to get to know my team, their strengths and where I could focus my efforts to assist the team in being successful. I made several changes in how work was received and distributed, revamped the RightFax system, wrote and developed new policies and procedures so the staff had clear directions on processes, and developed a staff recognition program. There was however still the great divide between the Atlanta office, which consisted of majority black staff and the Columbus office, which consisted of majority white staff. I made every effort to collaborate with the team there, which I had oversight of, but they were bent on trying to make the Atlanta team look less than capable. I prayed every day before entering the workplace for God to give me wisdom and allow me to have favor with man. God did just that with my staff VP, to whom I reported. She and I got along very well, and we were able to work closely together to try to bring some cohesiveness between the two offices. All our efforts were often futile and there were many days it was evident they didn't want any part of it. Sadly, enough there were even efforts to sabotage our credibility by notifying me perhaps five minutes before a big meeting that I needed to present some specific information to the team. Thanks be to God, I often was two to three steps ahead of them with the metrics already and was able to present without an issue. Praying for Godly wisdom daily always pays off. They didn't realize, I am a data driven person and try to always have my numbers ready to assess the team in reaching the stated goals.

I believe God places us in some settings so that we can be a voice for those who have no voice, especially when He places us in leadership roles. The team in Atlanta often felt under-appreciated, functioned with less than the needed resources and needed someone to listen to their concerns and effectively communicate the issues, backed up by data, and I saw myself as that person. After several months of exhausting all efforts to try to make brick without straw (achieve excellent results with fewer than needed resources), a consultant was asked to come in and assess the efficiency of my team and evaluate the effectiveness of the policies and procedures in place.

Being the people person that I am, I got along very well with the consultant and walked him through everything, not to brag but once

I know my stuff, its hard to throw me off. Well after the completion of the assessment, the consultant completed his report stating we needed an additional 12-14 nurses to adequately perform the duties within the standard timeframes, which is what I had been telling leadership all along, but as usual they must hear it from someone from the outside. Upon leaving, the consultant came to my office and asked if I would be interested in coming to work for him and his team, realizing my work ethic and operational skill set. His office was in Memphis and I had no interest in moving to Memphis, so I thanked him for the offer and awaited to hear from leadership their decision based upon his recommendations. Several weeks passed and finally the decision was that there would be no additional staff hired. I therefore had a decision to make and made an appointment to meet with one of the C-suite provider executives to discuss the matter at hand. I had always prided myself in making certain my team provided excellent customer service to the physicians and members we served, therefore, when we were unable to do so on a consistent basis it was time to have the critical conversation with the powers that be. It is always important to be prepared with factual data when presenting information to leadership in order to avoid sounding like you're just whining about poor results. I did just that and included the report from the outside consultant, which justified my findings of the need for additional staff to get the job done. To my amazement, after presenting all the information and advising the hold time for providers, which was close to two hours, this operational executive said to me that she didn't care how long the providers were on hold, we were not getting additional staff and that was that. So, I gathered my information and proceeded to return to my office. I communicated the events to my staff VP and she too was amazed. I therefore made up my mind that if the operational executive didn't care how long the providers were on hold and her salary was much higher than mine, why would I continue to beat my head up against the wall, trying to make it work. With that along with other corporate political issues that didn't seem to be getting better I decided it was time for me to move on.

I prayed about it that evening and proceeded to type my letter of resignation. I indicated that I was requesting my 13 weeks of severance pay, because I performed the job I was hired to do, relocating from Charleston to Atlanta only to find a work environment which was not conducive to fostering success but was complacent with failure. Since I was not accustomed to accepting failure, this was no longer the job for me. Being that I was voluntarily terminating my employment with the company, I had no way of knowing if the severance would be granted, but I wanted to give it a shot anyway. I had no other jobs lined up and I was a single woman with a mortgage and other expenses, yet there comes a time when you have peace to move on and this was one of those times. Well, I finished typing the letter and went to bed. In the middle of the night, the Holy Spirit woke me up and said *add to the letter "and all bonus dollars due you"*. I thought, now that's a stretch. I wasn't sure I would get the severance and now God you want me to add to the letter a request for bonus dollars also? Wow. Well I had to be obedient and I did just that. Believe it or not, HR complied with my request, and I received 13 weeks of my full salary and another $18K for pro-rated bonus dollars. One thing I can say about executive level bonuses, they are indeed a blessing, which I obviously worked for. The usual 60+ hour workweeks, the stress of driving for results with less than adequate resources, regulations that must be adhered to, audits from accrediting bodies, as well as the governmental agencies, are enough to justify every dollar received. I was so grateful the Holy Spirit woke me up and had me add the request for the bonus because that was money I could use for certain. I therefore worked with the team at Blue Cross Blue Shield of GA for almost two years. It was sad leaving my team, but I did what I was sent there to do and that was to reveal to leadership the needs of the team and implement as many corrective policies and procedures I could to make their lives a bit easier. It was now time to move on.

My next job in Atlanta was with Emory Crawford Long as a Clinical Coordinator. This job was a breath of fresh air because I worked a set number of hours, didn't have anyone reporting to me and I enjoyed being back in the hospital setting. I knew it was an interim position because my skill set is to lead operational teams, even though I'm a registered nurse. The previous several years were spent directing operational teams and I loved what I did. Nevertheless, one must do what they need to do until a better opportunity is presented. No matter what job I have, I plan to give it my all, 100%+ effort because it's a reflection of me and who's I am. I always reminded my team when I was director, I work as unto the Lord, even though I have a local boss, my ultimate boss is the Lord and I must function accordingly. This means being at work before time, as opposed to on time, ready to give my best effort to the tasks at hand. I think believers should be the best workers in any field of endeavor because we work as unto the Lord. Don't just do enough to get by, never going above and beyond. This is not who God called us to be. We are the head and not the tail, above and not beneath. If anyone should be excelling and advancing, the believers should be the ones.

It wasn't too many months later, I received a call from a company getting ready to start up a Medicaid program with the State of Georgia. I was very much interested in working with the Medicaid population because I felt like it gave purpose to my position, helping those less fortunate than myself. I interviewed for the position and was offered the job. I was very excited to be a part of a startup. I loved working with the VP of the program, Anne. She was a great leader and so down to earth. When I came on board the office didn't even have furniture, telephones, or cubicles built. There were a few nurses hired to assist with the start up, but it would be up to me to do the hiring, training, development of policies and procedures, as well as be the contact for the client representatives from the State for audits and reviews. I just loved it. I worked to hire the appropriate staff; I conducted training classes on the system, and developed all the policy and procedure documents based on the State's requirements for the program. We were able to obtain our Disease Management certification after only one year of operation, which was quite the feat and was later awarded another program to manage, which required hiring more staff, developing more policies and procedures and training the team. Even though it was an enormous amount of work, because the work environment was so great, it was a pleasure working there with leadership I could trust and had the staff's best interest, as well as the members we served. I worked for APS Healthcare for five years, developing some lasting friendships with my staff, supervisors who reported to me and contacts with other entities both within and outside of the company. Still to this day, I keep in touch with my Atlanta girls as I call them, which consists of two of the supervisors, Kim and Jacqui, who reported to me. Unfortunately, we loss one of our dear friends and team members, Sandra, to a heart attack a few years back. I really grew to love these ladies, even though we were in a boss, employee work relationship. It is possible to hold people to task respectfully and be friends with them outside of work, with no partiality. We had so many great memories over that five-year period and I would classify that job as one of my best positions ever.

It was during my tenure at APS Healthcare, one of my staff members introduced me to my future-second-husband, Page. My staff noticed that my life consisted of working and going to church, working and going to church. Often, on Fridays, they would ask, "Ms. Lynette what are your plans for the weekend?" I would usually say, "Not much, I may work some and will be going to church on Sunday." I loved going to New Birth. It operated with such a spirit of excellence and the campus would take your breath away. We often had very well-known guest preachers during conferences, to the likes of T. D. Jakes, Juanita Bynum, Myles Munroe, Keith Ellis, just to name a few, but from my perspective, they had nothing on Bishop Long. He was the humblest minister I had ever met, for the size of the church, which sat 10,000 in the main sanctuary and another several thousand in the overflow area. Even with that number of seats, we had two services and Bishop Long preached both services. He would sometimes even stand in the lobby to greet the members, which you rarely see ministers doing even with much smaller congregations. I witnessed so many awesome demonstrations of giving from the pulpit at New Birth I was constantly amazed. It was nothing to see single mothers receiving cars, members selected to have all their debt paid off, women in abusive situations being placed in apartments and removed from danger. Even though the church was huge, you still felt a sense of family and you would get to know the people who sat in the area where you would sit most Sundays and Wednesday nights. I'll never forget the level of giving and services provided for the people who had to flee New Orleans after hurricane Katrina. I volunteered in the family life center, which was turned into a mini Walmart for the people to shop for the items they needed without cost. I will never forget the Sunday, Bishop Long had a word of wisdom regarding a family whose house was about to go into foreclosure and he asked whoever the couple was to come forward. He also added that they had their paperwork regarding the foreclosure with them. This couple came down to the altar area and Bishop asked them how much it would take to get them out of foreclosure and they told him. He said to his staff, *take them in the back and get a check ready for them.* These were consistent experiences at New Birth, which I just loved seeing the hand of God in operation, meeting the needs of the people from the pulpit and not the people meeting the needs of those in the pulpit, which is much more commonplace. I also served on the outreach ministry team and had the opportunity to teach evangelism classes, as well. The homeless population in Atlanta was one of our focus areas and it blessed me tremendously to be able to feed and clothe these brothers and sisters monthly. I so appreciated the spiritual growth I experienced while attending New Birth. I was able to complete both my bachelor's and Master of Arts Degrees in Theology through the Life Christian University, which had a satellite campus located at New Birth. I have fond memories of New Birth and was saddened to hear of the death of Bishop Long early 2017. I had to make it a point to pay my respects and be in attendance at his funeral, which was fit for the great man of God that he was.

One day, one of my staff members asked if she could give a very nice gentleman she knew my work number for him to give me a call, so we could meet. I told her it was okay, and a couple of weeks passed, and I pretty much had forgotten about it when the phone rang, and this gentleman was on the other end. We exchanged our information and he agreed to call me that evening. He seemed very nice and I was impressed that according to my staff member, he was a minister. By now I had been divorced about nine years and it had been approximately four years since my heart was crushed due to the broken engagement to Nelson, but I'm always open to love and willing to give it another go.

He kept his word and called me that evening and we had a very good conversation. He ended the call with prayer, which really impressed me. Since he was a truck driver, who traveled Monday through Friday and home on the weekends, we didn't get to make plans to see each other for several days. In the interim, we talked on the phone each night and as always, he ended each call with prayer. Finally, we were able to make plans to meet each other at a restaurant, in the Stonecrest Mall area on Saturday evening. I got there early because I wanted to be there before he arrived, so I could see him when he came in and assess accordingly. When he arrived, I thought he was handsome. He was tall, with well-groomed gray hair, and he immediately made me laugh with something he said, which I can't remember verbatim now. It took the edge off the initial awkwardness when you first meet someone. We had a nice evening and agreed to see each other the next day, which was Sunday. From there, we talked on the phone every night and saw each other every weekend. He would attend church with me and things began to get serious quickly. Thankfully, he didn't believe in being intimate before marriage so that took the pressure off, but we knew we wouldn't be able to have a long dating relationship because we were both affectionate individuals. We started talking marriage a few months after dating. I met his family, who lived in Chicago and I took him to Charleston to meet my family and friends and everyone gave their approval.

The next step in the process was to go through marriage counseling, so we set up to meet with an Elder from New Birth, Elder Brenda Sims, who had her own pre-marital counseling service and performed weddings as well. We went through 13 weeks of counseling and thought we were ready to move to the next level and on Saturday, August 11, 2007, I entered holy matrimony with Page Atwater, at the Marriott Hotel in downtown Atlanta. It was a beautiful wedding, with a full bridal party and reception for approximately 125 guests. Family and friends came from Charleston SC, Chicago Illinois, which is where he was from and Elder Sims officiated the ceremony. Since I did not have a wedding the first time I got married, I wanted to have a formal wedding with all the trimmings. We had a live band and saxophonist and spent the honeymoon night in a penthouse suite at the Marriott. The next day we left for a five-day cruise to Mexico for our honeymoon. We were off to a pretty good start. We both were happy and got along very well. As we settled into our new lives together, I thought this is great. I've married a minister, we pray together, attend church together and he makes me laugh. Since I already had a 3,100 square foot home, and he had an apartment, it was clear that he would move in with me; however, I was not initially comfortable adding his name to the mortgage, and it may have been a point of contention for him. He said it was, but we did discuss it, and I expressed my views about it. I took into consideration that I have paid the mortgage on that house for four years at the time and if anything happened to me or us I didn't want any issues with his children having access versus my sons, who I had listed as beneficiaries up to that point. I know when you marry, everything should be joint, but I just didn't have a peace to do that so, it stayed that way.

We made it to our first anniversary and took a trip to Myrtle Beach to celebrate, which didn't go as well as planned. We got into a heated discussion about something, and I don't even remember what, but I am usually quick to forgive and move back to a happier place because life is too short. We made up and everything was fine.

As I mentioned, I loved going to New Birth Church, and he was fine with attending there when we met and after we married but then he said he wanted to find another church, and he didn't want to go to New Birth anymore. I was in shock, but, wanting to be a good wife, I conceded, and we visited a church one of my nurses at work recommended called New Life Church, where Pastor Marlin D. Harris was the Pastor. The first Sunday we attended, we loved the service, the teaching, and the music. I could see that they had an awesome outreach ministry, which was my passion. They would pick up men from the shelters on Saturday mornings, bring them to the church, feed them breakfast and then have classes on different topics and then provide them a bag lunch and take them back. They also had a clothes closet, from which the men could get clothing and they had a food pantry to serve the community as well. This hit all my criteria for ministry and we agreed that this would be our church after we had visited a couple of Sundays. We joined the church and attended their anniversary celebration the following Saturday evening. It really helped me to realize that this was a great ministry and I could settle in to moving forward with new members classes. God also made it clear to me one morning after I prayed by saying *you have been at New Birth for five years, now it's time for New Life.* This quickened in my spirit and I was now fully at peace with the move.

Several weeks prior my husband had received his layoff notice at work, stating they needed to lay off a few of the employees due to budget constraints. When he told me, I wasn't alarmed, because I earned a good income and had been taking care of the house by myself prior to us getting married so it would not be a strain for me to continue to do so. I suggested to him that since he was now 62, he could go ahead and retire and start drawing his social security as well as his other pension dollars. He could then start to move more into his ministry work and volunteerism. He agreed, and I thought we were set. During the same time, there was noise on my job with APS Healthcare, of new hires to take over the executive leadership roles. I was in the role of Chief Nursing Officer at the time, and the new person being hired was a PhD, in mental health and the other a Doctor of Chiropractic Medicine. I got along very well with the Doctor of Chiropractic Medicine. This person took over operational oversight, and the psychologist was to take over the area I previously had oversight of, and I would report to her. I had to train her in her new role, and it was a bit challenging in several ways, but I maintained my dignity and trained her to the best of my ability. This was a result of a change in our Executive Director, who wanted to bring in his own team, which is usually the case with a change at the top. I had staff come to me and say *they couldn't believe how well I handled that transition.* I would let them know, it was the grace of God that kept me balanced and in faith to endure the situation of training my boss. If I maintained my same paycheck, I was good.

Approximately two weeks after joining New Life Church, I came home from work on a Thursday only to find that my husband had cleared out the closets, drawers and storage of all his things and he was gone. I couldn't believe it. No warning, no major argument, nothing. That morning when I left for work we exchange pleasant greetings and I said have a blessed day, love you and he said you too, love you. It was amazing how I could feel something was off when I drove into the garage and his car wasn't there, but I said perhaps he went to the store or something and proceeded into the house. Once I went upstairs to our room to change clothes and saw his clothes gone, I couldn't breathe. I must have been having a panic attack. I called his sister and told her that he was gone and if she knew where he might be, but she was in shock as well. I tried to call his phone, no answer, no answer. My heart was racing, and

I was in total shock, hurt, confused, going through a myriad of emotions. I kept asking myself, what did I do? How could he do this to me? I was too embarrassed to tell my sons, best friends or anyone right away. I thought, maybe he will come back, it must be a misunderstanding. I tried to recall everything we said over that last several days. Did I say something wrong? Did I do something wrong? I could not come up with anything that would warrant him to just up and leave me like this. My emotions fluctuated between hurt and then anger trying to understand how he could do this. He knew it would rip my heart out of my chest. I did not sleep that night but still had to go to work the next day and try to put a smile on my face because I was not about to let my staff know my husband walked out and left me. We had this beautiful wedding and looked like the perfect couple, now this. How could this be? What is wrong with me, I asked myself? I can't ever seem to have a great relationship. I felt like I wanted to just disappear, never to return and face this horrible nightmare.

A couple of days later, he finally returned my call and said he would come by to talk. When he came in, I kept asking why? What had I done? He started to make up some crazy statements like, *I said his daughter wasn't going to pay back the money he sent her a few weeks ago, and that my son had worn a pair of his pants.* I was like, you must be kidding, right? That can not be the reason you left without notice, knowing how it would hurt me. I could not get a straight answer, and he kept stating he wasn't going to talk about it, that he was leaving. At that moment, I was so angry, this voice said to *get the butcher knife and stab him in the chest.* Oh, my goodness. Where did that come from? I didn't even know I could have such a thought. It was at that moment I understood how people can kill in the heat of an angry moment, especially if a gun is in the house. Thankfully, I did not act on the thought and just knowing I could have a thought like that put me in the bed the entire weekend. It took all that was within me to go to work the following Monday. I still had to act as if nothing was going on and take care of my business at work. When I arrived home each day, I pretty much cried myself to sleep. It's one thing to have a lot of arguments and then you break up, but when you don't and even exchange pleasantries the morning of the split, no one could see it coming. His sister was very sweet during this time and would check on my often and expressed her sorrow for what had happened. It wasn't until one of our post departure conversations did I find out he had been married five times prior to me. During our marriage counseling, he said he had been married only twice before; in actuality, he had been married five times, and I was his sixth wife. I asked his sister, why she didn't tell me that when we first spoke prior to us getting married? I recall her asking me if I knew he had been married before and I said I did, but that was with the thought of it only being twice before. In some way, it did make me feel a little better knowing this, because it showed me it wasn't me. He had some issues with lasting commitment. He had no problem getting married; he had problems staying married.

It took me a few weeks before I was even able to let my best friend, Barbara, know what happened and then I slowly began to let my other family members know. It took me a few months to let my staff and co-workers know. It was so sad. Everyone had been so happy for me getting married and I spent thousands of dollars on my dream wedding, only to have everything end in this horrible way. I was so hurt and embarrassed, harboring the thoughts of everyone thinking "what's wrong with her"? I must admit I did question God, in how could He allow this to happen? I'd been faithful and stood on His promise that if I delight myself in Him, He would give me the desires of my heart. How could He allow me to be shamed so publicly, again? First with the broken engagement and now another failed marriage. When the truth is told, it was none of God's doing because He does not force man to go against their will, but He does grace us to walk through what men do to us. I later began to realize what I was experiencing was a symptom of pride, to be so concerned about what people were thinking as opposed to me focusing solely on my emotional stability and taking care of my spiritual well-being.

It was interesting that my husband left approximately two weeks after we joined New Life Church, but I wanted to keep my commitment to this new ministry and I therefore stayed instead of returning to my beloved New Birth. I was glad I did because the Sunday I returned to church after my husband left, Pastor Harris began a series called "Finding God in the midst of your Pain". Oh, that message series was tailor made for me. It was based on the book, The Shack. God just bathed my heart each week, as I sat in church listening and crying. The series lasted six weeks and the Tuesday night after that last message in the series, I was standing in church during the worship service and the Lord spoke to my heart saying, *Lynette, what the enemy says about you, is that if he can get the right person(s) to reject you, he wants you to lose your faith in God.* It was at that moment, it all became clear to me and the strength of the Lord rose up on the inside of me and I said, "Devil, you're a liar. I don't care who comes and who goes, I will not lose my faith in God. I know God is a good God and I can trust Him with my life." It was after that encounter I began to stand strong in my faith in God and it spoke comfort to my soul and spirit. My night was long, but I stood on the promise that weeping endures for a night, but joy comes in the morning. I began to see the beauty of the sunshine and knew I was going to be all right.

I even had the courage to have a conversation with my husband and expressed my disappointment in him but knew that I had been a good wife and he had messed with God's daughter and he would reap the consequences of his actions, but I forgave him and was moving on with my life. I waited the standard one year and then filed for divorced, which was finalized within three months of filing. By then, he had returned to Chicago, I mailed him our final divorce decree, and I closed that chapter in my life.

I never intended to be divorced twice, but this was the hand I was dealt, and I have had to make the best of it and reclaim my joy and peace amid life happening each day. As I look back over that time, I don't harbor any ill feelings toward Page, since I should have done my due diligence in researching his background and not let the title "minister" fool me into thinking he was good for me. Just because he prayed with me at the end of every call, honored God with regards to maintaining celibacy before our marriage, it didn't mean his head was in the right place. He later acknowledged that I was a good wife and that God really dealt with him harshly because of what he did to me. I refused to allow the root of bitterness to grow in my heart and vowed to be better and not bitter. I vowed to be better in tuned with what's good for me and my life, as well as understanding the true character and heart of a man and not just his spiritual status. I believe many women have made the mistake of limiting their criteria to the man being "saved". Well its more to a man's character than his eternal salvation. His spirit may be saved but if his mind and emotions are messed up you still don't have heaven on earth with a person. One of the enemy's tools is to hurt children at a young age, so their mind and emotions are so negatively impacted it affects their adult life. People must take the time to be delivered from things which happened to them in their past and understand how it may have affected them. My husband shared with me how he had been molested by a woman when he was around 10 years old, and I know it had an impact on him, because he still mentioned it in his 60's. There is a reason he had been married six times, including me, and continues to marry (he has since married again after our divorce). It is not normal and needs to be dealt with but, fortunately for me, it's his and his new wife's issue to deal with and not mine. I don't mean to sound callous, but one can only suggest counseling to someone, so they can be delivered, but if they don't see the need then there's nothing you can do.

Around November 2009, I started desiring to return home to Jacksonville, Florida. I realized I was maturing and wanted to spend more time around my family. I had been gone from Jacksonville since 1977 and I knew a lot would have changed since then, but I was longing for home. I therefore, updated my resume and placed it on the appropriate recruiting websites. I was first contacted by a recruiter regarding a job in Tampa Florida. It was a start-up Medicaid plan, like the plan I worked with for APS Healthcare. I drove to Tallahassee Florida to meet with the newly hired executive director and another executive and felt good about the interview meeting. I few days later, I received a call from the recruiter and they wanted to make me an offer. I listened intently to the details and it appeared some things had changed from the original discussion, so I advised that I would pray about it over the weekend and get back with them on the following Monday. During the weekend, as I prayed intermittently about it, I did not have a peace to accept the position. So, I called them on Monday morning to let them know my decision, which clearly disappointed them. I felt it important to have a peace about such an important move and since my desire was to move back to Jacksonville and this offer was for Tampa, I did not feel led to accept it.

In January, I received a call from a recruiter about a director level position that opened in Jacksonville, Florida, and they wanted me to come down for an interview. I was thrilled and grateful that I had not accepted the position previously offered in Tampa. God knew this position was coming open and didn't allow me to have peace about accepting the other offer. He is indeed a good Father God. I made the necessary plans to travel to Jacksonville for the interview and was able to stay with my nieces during the quick trip. The interviews lasted approximately six hours because I met with several leaders and decision makers. I can usually tell how well the interviews are going because of the responses received from the interviewers and I could tell this was going to be my next job. After my interview ended with the Chief Medical Officer, at 6:00 p.m. I felt good about landing the position. A few days later, I received the call from their human resource department with an offer and I happily accepted, ready to start my transition back to Florida. So, in February 2010, I would be starting my new role as Director of Clinical Review for Florida Blue insurance company in Jacksonville Florida.

Return to Jacksonville

Oh, back where it all began or at least where I was born. It was great to be back home and closer to family members, which included by youngest sister, Annette, my two brothers, Ronald and Donald, my nieces, nephews, cousins and my last living Aunt Viola. I was hoping to reconnect with all of them because I had been away for over 44 years.

I rented a one-bedroom apartment down the street from my new job, which made it very convenient, especially since I was again learning my away around the city. Apartment living is not my favorite form of living but this one was in a great location and had its perks like daily trash pick-ups, a beautiful view of the pond, and close to the St. John's Towne Center for shopping. I settled in quickly and went through the initial challenges of a new position at the Director level, which included long hours getting to know the lay of the land, staff, leaders, processes, external partners, computer systems, and most importantly, what it would take to be successful in my new role.

I really enjoy managing operations and find it rewarding when I can find new ways to build efficiencies, reduce cost, drive to results and meet the needs of my team all in a day's work. If only it were that simple, but honestly my adrenalin was always running high, which I didn't mind if I could see progress being made. It took a while, but after many hours of focus, collaboration with staff and other business partners and stakeholders, I would like to think I brought positive energy to my role and the organization benefited from me being there. Although there was quite a bit of senior leadership turn over, our team survived and thrived. Much was accomplished, and I grew both professionally and emotionally during my tenure. God allowed me to meet, lead and mentor some wonderful people, as well as being led by some strong women leaders.

After working with the organization for approximately seven years, it was clear to me that my time in this career field was over. I knew this after an interesting turn of events.

I always juggled several projects at one time, but it became clear to me that the number of hours I had to put in to effectively manage it all was not the life I wanted to continue to live. It was a Thursday evening in August 2016, and I was leaving the office around 8:00 p.m., but knew I still needed to go to the gym to workout, which I did. On my way home from the gym, I began to just cry out to God that I needed a change and that I was tired. Tears were rolling down my face like waterfalls and I knew this was one of those serious conversations with God, along with the ugly cry. As I pulled into my subdivision and stopped to get the mail, I noticed I had a voicemail on my cellphone, so I decided to listen prior to getting my mail. Upon listening to the voicemail, I heard a dear young lady with whom I had prayed with several weeks ago, thanking me for my prayer and explaining how she put into action what we spoke about during our last call and how grateful she was for me. She stated that her family was doing great and she just felt led to call me and say thank you. Well, hearing this caused me to go into the ugly cry again. I sat in my car weeping and then I heard the Spirit of the Lord say to me *You see you are not in your true purpose. You are to help*

*others, but you have exhausted all your energy and effort doing a
job, for what reason?*

After hearing this, it felt like a 200-pound weight had been lifted
off my shoulders and I knew what I had to do. Make the transition.
I didn't have any concrete plans but knew it was time for me to
move on, to what I didn't know. I believe there are times when God
will not show you the next step until you take the first step, which
for me was deciding to retire from my current role as Director of
Clinical Review.

On Friday morning, I arrived at work early and reached out
to the retirement representative with the organization and my
investment company to verify 401K benefits. Everything seemed in
order, and I felt good about the decision I was about to make. I was
truly at peace about it and had not felt so sure about something in
quite some time. Being the planner that I am, I still laid out how I
would cover expenses until I filed for retirement benefits when I
turned 62 the following February 2017. Over the weekend, I typed
my letter of resignation for both my VP and Senior Director and
emailed it to them on Sunday evening with a follow up meeting
scheduled for early Monday morning. I also made plans to notify the
Chief Medical Officer, the Medical Directors, my direct reports and
then all my staff, which were located throughout the State, shortly
thereafter. I set up calendar appointments to meet with each of
them and looked forward to notifying every one of my plans.

Monday morning could not come soon enough, but once it did,
I arrived at work early and began the notifications as I had planned.
I shared my testimony of how the decision came about to retire; I
knew it was the right thing to do, because I didn't get emotional
during my meetings, which is not like me. I don't mind shedding
heartfelt tears and being vulnerable with my team and others for

whom I care about, but this time was different. I was at peace, and this was the decision God wanted me to make. I was so sure of my decision, I gave only a two-week notice, which would have been at least a month notice for a director level position under different circumstances. However, when its time to go, you need to go. Staying longer just delays the next steps in your journey.

Over the next two weeks, I notified all my business partners throughout the organization, as well as external partners, of my decision to retire and move to the next chapter of my life. I transitioned projects to appropriate individuals and summarized accomplishments of my team up to that point in the yearly review process, sharing it with my senior leadership so it would be clear the state in which I left the department.

So, on Thursday, September 1, 2016, I carried all the remnants of my employment with Florida Blue to my car for the last time. As I was leaving, I was reminded to be grateful for all the experiences, both good and challenging, which occurred over the last seven years since each one added to my life's story and prepared me for what God had in store for my future.

Approximately two weeks after retiring, I received an email from a lady named Janet Atwood regarding the Passion Test. It sounded very intriguing since it related to identifying your top five passions, so you could live your purpose. I thought it very timely and knew that nothing happens by chance and it was meant for me to receive this email. I had no way of knowing how Ms. Attwood knew my email address or anything about me, but at this point it didn't matter because I just knew that in God all these things were working together for my good.

I responded to the email and registered to take this passion test, so I could identify my top 5 passions and ensure I was about to live my true purpose. Within a few days, I was contacted by one of the facilitators, and she walked me through the process and I identified what was important to me and how my life aligned or didn't align with those passions. I found the process to be very thought provoking and it challenged me to dig deep to really get clear on what I was passionate about, since those are the clues to my destiny and purpose. At the end of the process, I realized that my passions centered on service, making a difference in the lives of others, teaching, and supporting the homeless. I realized however, my life was not aligned with making those things a priority, which I knew I had to change. At the end of the course, I was offered the opportunity to take a four-day course to become a facilitator of the passion test also, which I found to be very exciting and in alignment with my desire to teach and make a difference in the lives of others.

Here was an opportunity being presented to me that I could see the hand of God orchestrating, so I agreed to do it. I participated in the four-day training along with 16 other participants from around the world via the Zoom meeting technology. It was an awesome experience meeting people from Saudi Arabia, China, Finland, Denmark, Mexico, Canada, UK, Australia, and two other States within the United States. Over the four-day period, we practiced facilitating the course and had a lot of fun doing so. It was such an enriching experience and it taught me a lesson in understanding that people are people no matter where they are from and all have something to contribute to our life experiences.

Following the course, which included instructions on how to start a business by facilitating the passion test, I knew it was my time to do something I had always wanted to do, start a business. During the same time, I was engaged in taking the course; I was given the opportunity to become an honorary member of a wonderful professional organization called We Are Women in Business, even though at the time I didn't have a business established. It was the inspiration of these wonderful ladies, along with the prompting of the Holy Spirit aligning everything, the time was right for me to move forward and in December 2016, I launched Purpose Made Alive, LLC, my first business.

I secured my tax ID, Limited Liability Corporation designation, registered the organization, paid my business taxes, worked with my sons to develop a logo, website, business cards and contracted with a graphic designer to develop a brochure about my offerings, before the end of the year. Record timing, which confirmed this was the direction I needed to move. With those things completed, I conducted my first workshop on Saturday, January 21, 2017 in my beloved Charleston SC among friends and supporters, with an awesome turnout and feedback. I love to facilitate and inspire people to live their best lives, which this allowed me to do. What a win, win. My next two workshops were conducted in Atlanta and Jacksonville, both with great response and turnout. I felt great about my decision to move forward with this endeavor and knew God had placed His seal of approval on it.

It's important to always remember, even though God approves of what we set our hands to do, He does not promise it will always be easy. Anything worth doing will take work, preparation and engagement with others. The remainder of the year required that I shift the location of the workshop from the usual hotels, to my home, when necessary and I made the adjustment and followed through to meet the needs of my participants. I am excited to see where God will lead me as I continue to pursue this endeavor and plan to expand the business to the next level of engagement, strategically targeting the most appropriate audiences.

Marriage #3

After surviving two divorces, I didn't know if I would ever marry again, although I always desired to be married, to have a mutual loving relationship with someone. I refused to allow bitterness to take root in my heart, even after the devastating experience of my second marriage and broken engagement prior to that. Instead, I remained open to love, even when there were no signs of it finding me. I had grown from my experiences and understood the importance of really getting to know someone for real, which could not take place within six months of meeting them. This was my usual time limit for dating to avoid fornicating but learned the hard way that this standard was not enough time, regardless of my age. Now that I was settled into my new life in Jacksonville, I decided to become a member of a single's dating service called, Singles Plus. It required a three-hour in person interview, psychological testing, credit check, background check and came with a hefty price tag. Since my life consisted of mainly work and church at the time, I didn't often find myself in an environment of mature available men to ask me out on a date. One would think church would be the ideal place to meet mister right, but I found most men in church don't want to date other ladies in their church because things can become very awkward in the event you go your separate ways. Therefore, when I was contacted by this organization, the process sounded like a viable option.

The first three dates they connected me with were not my type. I always remained polite and respectful but let them know quickly I was not interested in a second date. I didn't see the need to prolong the inevitable and I never liked leading people on. Then the fourth person they connected me with was my now beloved husband, Larry Lewis. When I received the email giving me his attributes, I was glad to see that he was also a registered nurse, which would allow us to have that in common along with love of theater, travel and adventure. We spoke initially on the phone and agreed to meet at the Conch House in St. Augustine, which would be mid-way between where he lived and where I lived. At the time, he lived in Palm Coast and I lived in Bartram Park, near the start of St. Johns County. Our first date went very well, and he impressed me with his sense of humor, ease of conversation and warm soul. I left the first date thinking, okay, I like this one. We'll see where it leads. We dated for approximately six months and somehow my internal six-month clock tried to kick in and we decided to put a hold on the relationship for a while after a trip to Tampa in August, even though I knew I really liked this guy.

For the next few months, we did not communicate with each other even though I thought about him often. When October rolled around, I decided to send him a birthday card, which caused him to give me a call to thank me for the card. With that call we started to slowly begin communicating again but not every day and met only occasionally for a date here and there. I did notice this time; however, our intentions were more deliberate because we both knew there was something special about our relationship, but we wanted to take it slow and engage in deeper conversations about our thoughts, feelings, and beliefs. There was one thing that always stood out to me regarding him; it was the way in which he treated me. He always made me feel special and safe, which is something I had longed to feel in a relationship all my life. He was considerate with reference to being timely for our dates and if he was going to be late, which rarely happened, he would always let me know prior to the expected arrival time. He made every effort to plan things for us to do, which was new for me because in previous relationships and marriages, I had to do all the planning and coordinating anything other than eating out. I appreciated him planning things with me that I had never done before such as touring St. Augustine from above in a helicopter and riding the coastline on a motorcycle, with helmet on of course. He owned his own home in Palm Coast and was conscientious in making sure his bills were paid as evident by a credit score of 800+, which I didn't see in my second husband.

This caused me to re-evaluate that list we ladies often have, and I know there are mixed views on this. Some would say, *girl, don't settle, ask God for what you want and don't accept anything less.* They fail to tell you that God may not have approved our list and He often disguises our blessings, so He can see if our heart is pure and open to the process. I believe I made that mistake with my engagement and second husband, being awe struck because they had the title of Pastor and minister in front of their names, yet neither even came close in character to Larry, so there is more to it than only being spiritually minded in finding a suitable mate.

About one and half years into our relationship, Larry decided to take a nursing job in Jacksonville, selling his home in Palm Coast and purchasing a condo in the Baymeadows area on the Southside. This allowed us to spend more time together and our relationship began to blossom. All the while, I was thanking God for bringing this wonderful man into my life. We came from different backgrounds since he was not raised in the church, but I loved the way he realized the need to make the necessary changes to win me as his wife. For the first time I felt like I was the prize instead of me trying to convince someone I was the prize. He recognized my value and treated me accordingly. It is a true statement that a real man knows when he has a good woman and if they really love you they will do what needs to be done to ensure they keep you. We as females are typically reciprocal individuals and respond according to how we are treated. When the man goes out of his way to demonstrate his love for us, we go out of our way to respond to that love.

After three and a half years of commitment to take the time to understand each other's makeup and true character, Larry and I entered holy matrimony on Wednesday, September 6th, 2017 at Sandals Resort in Barbados West Indies. It was a beautiful ceremony designed just for the two of us, which made it even more special. It wasn't that we didn't care about our family and friends but decided for this one, it needed to be just the two of us. No performance for anyone, no catering to anyone else's needs or expectations, jut the two of us. The resort was gorgeous, and they catered to our every need and made our day very special. It was one of the best days of my life and I will cherish it in my heart for the rest of my life.

Although the wedding was private, we did, however, plan a nice dinner celebration upon our return home for our children and grandchildren in Jacksonville in a private dining room at Brio's Restaurant in the St. John's Towne Center. My husband Larry has two children, the oldest being his daughter, Laquita, who's married to Emanuel and they have four children, Octavia, John, Larry and Deadra, the youngest is his son Chris, with his significant other Brandy and their have three sons, Justin, Chris Jr. and Carter. I have two sons, the oldest being Derrick Joyce, engaged to Stacey, and he has two sons Ahmad and Derrick Jr.; Stacey has two sons, Jareese and Keon. My youngest is Chris Joyce, who's married to Latia, and they have two children, Jeriah and Amariah. We had a beautiful celebration with our families, and it allowed everyone to come together, some for the first time, but everyone got along very well. It did our hearts good to see and experience the togetherness even for a few days. We are looking forward to more family times in the future.

My Spiritual Journey

My spiritual journey started at the age of five, when I accepted Jesus into my heart and made Him the Lord of my life, receiving His forgiveness for my sins. I was baptized by the Reverend Dallas Graham, at Mt. Ararat Baptist Church in Jacksonville Florida. I loved going to church. I loved everything about it from the singing, marching of choirs and usher boards to the preaching and teaching.

For some reason, I always felt older than my stated age and seemed to understand things very early in life, so even though I was only five years old, I understood fully what I did and prayed a lot growing up because of all the things I endured. We moved from Florida when I was eight years old so the second church I attended was in Philadelphia. It was a smaller church than Mt. Ararat, but the size didn't really matter to me. I just enjoyed being there. During those days, the churches had Sunday school and I would get up early, so I could make it to Sunday school, even when no one else in my family planned to attend on any given Sunday. I didn't want to miss church. It was my lifeline in a sense and definitely got me out of the house and away from my brother before he could think of some way to hurt me. I really liked knowing the answers to questions asked about the Bible stories the teacher read to us. These were things I felt I could control and it carried over into my schoolwork as well. I thrived on getting good grades, being seen as a good student and overall good person. When I think back on this I imagine it gave me some comfort to be seen in a positive way rather than hated by my own brother.

Years passed, and I followed the same pattern wherever we moved in Philadelphia until I finished high school and started college. It was during that period of time, when I stopped attending church and felt the need to taste the freedom of being on my own, partying to be social and indulging in behaviors I knew didn't serve me well. I always held the thoughts of God in the back of my mind and heart, but they weren't a priority for me at the time. That all changed the night I had the encounter with the Spirit of the Lord after smoking marijuana (pot/weed) with this guy, I barely knew. I believe the Lord snatched me out of the enemy's grip when He warred for my soul and allowed me to have that out of body experience while He cleaned me up from the inside out. To this day, I have never touched weed again. Returning to church with my friend, Annette, the following Sunday after that experience, set me on the path back to putting God first in my life. I am so glad it did.

Not too long after that I returned to Jacksonville the first time and started my life there with one thing leading to another such as employment, dating, marriage, miscarriage, birth of son and relocating to Charleston, South Carolina.

I would say I matured the most spiritually while living in Charleston, South Carolina, because I was hungry to know God more and in a deeper way. I attended bible studies, revivals, conferences and any other service that I thought would enrich my knowledge in the things of God. I used to sit in my bedroom mediating and trying to let my mind think back to the time prior to God speaking the world into existence. God was there, but all that we see now, was not. I tried to imagine what that must have been like, but my mind could not comprehend it. I used to ask God questions like,

"If Romans 10: 9 – 10, is how we are saved, how then do babies that die at birth or miscarry go to heaven since they did not have a chance to confess Christ and repent for sins, especially since we were shapen in iniquity and in sin did our mothers conceive us (Psalm 51:5)? I searched scriptures for answers to questions that I dared not discuss with other people in the event they wouldn't understand. Things like, Luke 10:17-20 where Jesus told the seventy disciples when they returned from ministry not the be excited about demons being subject unto them but rejoice because their names are written in heaven. I tried to understand how this could be when Jesus had not yet died and rose again for their sins, yet He said their names were already written in heaven at the time He was talking to them. Could it be that at the point of conception their names were written, which would justify babies going to heaven when they die at birth? Jeremiah states that He, God knew us before we were formed in our mother's womb. Another scripture that tied into this thought is Revelation 3:5 where Jesus said He will not blot out his name from the Book of Life but will confess his name before my Father and before His angels, which means the names must already be there in order to possibly be blotted out. Then when you look at Revelation 17:8 *"The beast that you saw was and is not and will ascend out of the bottomless pit and go to perdition. And those who dwell on the earth will marvel, whose names are not written in the Book of Life from the foundation of the world, when they see the beast that was and is not and yet is."* This lets us know there are those whose names were not written, but could it be because God is all knowing and knows who will be saved. Questions of whether God, being a just God, allows the world in, unless they opt out by rejecting Jesus Christ prior to the end of their life. Since babies don't reject Christ, they would automatically be in. I realized that it is important not to take scripture out of context and some questions would be answered only when I see Jesus. I am grateful however that my understanding of receiving Jesus as my Lord and Savior and making Him Lord of my life and walking in righteousness is based on the price He paid with His blood for my sins to be forgiven. This I can stand on and is my hope of glory.

The following churches all shaped my spiritual journey over the years and collectively deposited many, many nuggets of spiritual truths into my life. They are: Pilgrim Baptist Church under Minister Frederick Hilton as the Bible Study minister; Eastside Baptist Church under Pastor Alex Capers; Glad Tidings Assembly of God under Pastor Ernest Oliver; Full Gospel Faith Tabernacle under Pastor Clifford Whitfield; Lord of the Harvest Christian Faith Center under Pastors Steven and Marlene Williams all of Charleston SC; New Birth Missionary Baptist Church under the late Bishop Eddie L. Long; New Life Church under Pastor Marlin D. Harris both of Atlanta Georgia; Faith Christian Center now Impact Church, under Bishop George and Pastor April Davis of Jacksonville Florida.

I'm grateful for the service opportunities presented to me over the years to serve in various capacities to build the Kingdom of God on the earth and serve the people of God. This included elementary and high school Sunday School teacher, BTU Leader, Praise and Worship leader, Director of Boys & Girls Missionary Crusade, leader for Youth Choir, Director of Outreach Ministry, Director of Singles Ministry, ordained Elder and licensed minister of the Gospel, instructor at Holy Spirit Bible College, instructor of Evangelism at New Birth, altar call team administrator, coordinator for an in-school food pantry and weekly Reading Pals volunteer.

Remaining open to the Spirit of the Lord as He orders my steps is a key focus at this season in my life. It's always interesting and sometimes challenging when transitioning from a place where you were a known leader to a place where no one knows your name. I remind myself that my gifts will make room for me and that the gifts are given without repentance so at the right time and during the right season God will allow me to move in my gifting with a greater anointing than ever before. In the meantime, I will continue to walk in preparation for the appointed time.

Purpose, Pain's Promise

The Word of God tells us in, John 16:33b that *"in the world we shall have tribulation but be of good cheer because I, Jesus have overcome the world."* Although we experience pain, purpose is the ultimate promise for the pain experienced. 2 Corinthians 4:17 states. *"for our light affliction which is but for a moment, is working for us a far more exceeding and eternal weight of glory".*

We all have a past, but our prayer must be for God to show us who He created us to be before the pain of the:

- molestation
- physical, emotional abuse
- abortion
- miscarriage
- divorce(s)
- job loss
- rejection

or whatever your pain stemmed from. The voices will try to continue to label us with the list of painful experiences, as if we're damaged goods, but God will help us to distinguish between what has happened to us and who we are. God wants us to know that we can bring our brokenness to Him, so He can love us back into the person who existed before the knowledge of pain ever existed in our lives, an innocent child loved unconditionally by a nurturing

Father, God.

We must pray to let go of the guilt and shame, who we think we ought to be and let God show us our identity, not the one given to us by our earthly fathers, but the identity that only God can give us, sons and daughters of the most-high God.

I am not talking about any God; I'm talking about the God that stepped out of eternity into time to demonstrate His love for us. The one who told the oceans how far they could roll onto the shoreline, the one who spoke the world into existence and said that we are fearfully and wonderfully made. That God loves us more than our minds can comprehend, and our hearts can perceive for He tells us in Psalm 34:18 in the Message Bible: *"If your heart is broken, you'll find God right there; if you're kicked in the gut, he'll help you catch your breath"*. That's my God.

I remember when my sister was hit in the stomach with a baseball bat by a mean little boy in our neighborhood in Philadelphia, and she couldn't catch her breath. I think of that story when I read that scripture because all she needed was to catch her breath but instead she had to be taken to the hospital. God is saying, I am your rescuer and I will help you catch your breath when life kicks you in the gut. Whether we like it or not, in this life we will have tribulation, someone or something will kick us in the gut, but thanks be to God, He's here to help us catch our breath.

The promise of our painful experiences is to reveal the essence of the real you. All the layers of pain, guilt, shame and frustrations are pulled back, and God says, "that woman", "that man" is worth every drop of blood I shed to make them whole. He wants us to walk in that wholeness, that unique purpose for which He created us. Those painful experiences molds and shapes us into the purposeful existence, which allows us to be sensitive to and serve others who have gone through similar experiences.

Second Corinthians 1:3 – 4 states, *"Blessed be God, even the Father of our Lord Jesus Christ, the Father of mercies, and the God of all comfort; Who, comforts us in all our tribulation, that we may be able to comfort them which are in any trouble, by the comfort wherewith we ourselves are comforted of God."*

This has purpose associated with it because out of our tribulation comes a message and service to others for their comfort.

My family was once homeless, living in a hotel or with other people who were kind enough to take us in; therefore, pain's promise is my purpose to meet the needs of the homeless and serve them however, I can.

Growing up, I desperately needed someone to love me and make a difference in my life, therefore, pain's promise is my purpose to make a difference in the lives of others through service and education. So, I volunteer to help educate four-year old's, so they learn to read, and I mentor and speak into the lives of young ladies so that their life may be better.

I know what it is to be hungry and eat cornbread for a week, so pain's promise is my purpose to serve others by heading up a food pantry and providing groceries to needy families.

I know what it is to grow up with no passion due to the pain of abuse and low self-esteem, therefore, pain's promise is my purpose to inspire others to live a passionate life on purpose and not by accident.

God does not waste one painful experience we have endured during our lifetime. I'm reminded of when I was in the second grade and had the need to use the restroom really bad, but the teacher kept ignoring my raised hand. So, I walked up to her desk and stood next to her and asked if I could please go to the restroom, but she told me to go sit down. Well, it was too late, the floodgates opened and there was a puddle on the floor. I proceeded to knock over the trashcan, so it would appear to my classmates that there was water running out of the trash can. I'm not sure why I thought to do that, but I did. She realized that I really had to go to the bathroom then and sent me to the office. I was so embarrassed, especially when the entire class started laughing. Many years later when I was volunteering in an elementary school, I was walking down the hall and this sweet little girl was walking down the hall crying her little eyes out. She was so tiny, around 4 or 5 years old. I stopped to ask her what was wrong, and she said, *"I wet myself"*. I gave her a big hug and said *"it's okay, do you know I did the same thing when I was a little girl. Let's go to the office and get you some dry clothes. Everything is going to be alright."*

Now that might seem like a small thing, but I can image how it made her feel to have this grown woman acknowledge her pain and share my story that I had done the same thing. I'm sure it caused her to feel a little better about the situation. I would have loved to have someone say that to me when I was in the second grade, but that wasn't my story. Yet, the key is that the painful experience was not wasted, because I was able to comfort this child because of what I experienced.

Therefore, each painful experience God allows us to survive and thrive in, takes us to the other side and shifts us into purpose. Let's be clear, purpose is not our careers, although our career can fit into our purpose. Purpose is not what we can do to get ahead, make a name for ourselves, or secure the future for us, our four and no more. Purpose is more about the collective unique experiences, talents and gifts we bring and share with others to make the world a better place. We attained those unique attributes through a myriad of life's experiences including wins-losses, good-bad decisions, successful triumphs and painful defeats. Therefore, I know *purpose, is pain's promise*. I am living it each day as I journey into destiny, knowing the pain and scars of my past are fading into a purposeful future.

About the Author

Lynette Lewis is the owner and CEO of Purpose Made Alive, LLC, a facilitation and motivational speaker services company. She is a retired registered nurse executive, with over 40 years of experience in corporate healthcare management and a proficiency in Christian ministry as a licensed and ordained minister with a Master of Arts in Theology from Life Christian University. She has been recognized by both Metropolitan and Empire Who's Who of Executives and Professionals for her outstanding leadership and has received numerous awards for her service and commitment to churches, organizations and communities. She is a Certified Technical Trainer and Certified Facilitator of the Passion Test®, a tool used to help individuals identify their top 5 passions, which are the clues to their destiny and purpose. She has facilitated the Passion Test workshop in Jacksonville Florida, Charleston South Carolina and Atlanta Georgia and received excellent feedback from participants regarding this life changing experience. She has been featured twice in the *Program Success* magazine, recognizing women in business.

As a servant leader, she feels it's extremely important to give back to the community in the tangible form of service in an effort to make a difference in the lives of others. She is the coordinator of the In-school Food Pantry at Woodland Acres Elementary School serving the families of the Arlington area of Jacksonville Florida and is a weekly Reading Pal volunteer since its inception in 2012, with the United Way of Northeast Florida. She serves as Chaplin for a women's professional organization, We Are Women in Business and is a member of the Family Strengthening workgroup of Arlington 20/20 of Revitalize Arlington Community Development. She is a faithful member of Impact Church in Jacksonville Florida, under the leadership of Bishop George Davis and Pastor April Davis.

Mrs. Lewis' purpose statement is *to make a difference in the lives of others through service, education and inspiration, to help people identify their passions so they can live their purpose.* She resides in Jacksonville Florida with her husband, Larry Lewis, and is the mother of two adult sons, Derrick D. Joyce and Christopher D. Joyce, aka Choyce and daughter-in-law, Latia V. Joyce. She is the proud grandmother of Ahmad Nealy, Derrick Joyce, Jr., Jeriah Joyce, and Amariah Joyce and great-grandmother of Jaevion Nealy.

Services Available by Purpose Made Alive, LLC.

Facilitation of 30-minute Passion & Purpose Presentation

Facilitation of 3-hour Passion Test Workshop

Servant Leadership Presentation

Significance of Purpose Presentation

Motivational & Inspirational Speaker services for:

Women's Conferences

Church Groups

Sorority Groups

Family Reunions

College Classes

Special Events

Contact Information for bookings:
Website: www.PurposeMadeAlive.com
Email: purposemadealive@gmail.com

References

- Center for Disease Control, Atlanta Georgia
- The New King James version Bible
- The Message Bible

Made in the USA
Lexington, KY
29 December 2018